The Time of the Messiah

A Prophetic Picture of the End-Time Church

The Time of the Messiah

A Prophetic Picture of the End-Time Church

by Kelley Varner

 Unless otherwise identified, Scripture quotations are from the authorized King James Version (KJV). Scriptures marked NIV are from the New International Version®. NIV®. Copyright ©, 1973, 1978, 1984 by International Bible Society. Scriptures marked (TLB), (ASV), (NKJ), and (AMP) are taken from The Living Bible, the American Standard Version, the New King James Version, and the Amplified Bible, respectively. Scripture quotes are also taken from the Moffatt, Phillips, and Jerusalem Bible translations as indicated.

Take note that the name satan and related names are not capitalized. We choose not to acknowledge him, even to the point of violating grammatical rules.

Destiny Image® Publishers, Inc.
P.O. Box 310
Shippensburg, PA 17257-0310

"Speaking to the Purposes of God for This Generation and for the Generations to Come"

ISBN 1-56043-177-6

For Worldwide Distribution
Printed in the U.S.A.

Acknowledgments

To all the local churches and individuals whose gifts made this project possible.

To Pastor Michael A. Smith, Victory Fellowship, West Memphis, Arkansas, for sharing the inspired words to his song, "He's Not Just a Baby Anymore...."

To the Holy Spirit, who is my Teacher.

Dedication

Jn. 1:6, KJV

There was a man sent from God....

These are days of global harvest. God has graciously brought His people out of Egypt and through the wilderness; we have experienced the blood of the Lamb in Passover and the power of His Spirit in Pentecost. As we stand postured to enter our land of providential promise, to partake of the fullness of the Feast of Tabernacles, the words of the apostle Paul ring louder than ever:

1 Cor. 4:15, KJV

For though ye have ten thousand instructors in Christ, yet have ye not many fathers....

The contemporary American Church, my generation, was born in the wild. We desperately need seasoned fathers like Caleb and Joshua to arise, to encourage and inspire us to cross the Jordan that we might possess our predetermined destiny.

Like Caleb, Apostle G.C. McCurry has been preserved unto this generation. For over half a century, he has faithfully proclaimed the Word of the Lord to the Body of Christ. Like Joshua, he has caused many others to inherit.

Before the Ark of the Covenant was brought into the view of the entire nation and ultimately found its final resting place in Zion, it was kept safe in the house of faithful Obed-edom. The mysteries of the Kingdom have been tucked away in the hearts of faithful apostolic and prophetic men and women for decades. Now it is time to favor Zion, to declare present truth to all men.

Throughout the 1970s, Prophet Bill Britton taught me how to write, but Apostle G.C. McCurry showed me how to preach.

Thank you, Pastor McCurry, for taking time to impart the Word of the Lord to my life. Wherever my voice is heard, your voice is heard. I give honor to whom honor is due.

About the Cover

Designing this cover initially presented me with some unique challenges. I wanted to portray Christ's coming as the divine Seed, but I also wanted to picture Him as the King. Because I like to present things in a non-traditional manner, I wanted to establish an image that would subtly convey each of these elements.

After praying for direction, an image flashed into my mind—the image you now see on the cover of this book. The crown signifies the King coming forth out of the ground as a seed. The path represents His journey back to the mountain of God. The light from Heaven reminds us of the Father's declaration, "...This is My beloved Son..." (Mt. 3:17b) and that "...[the fields] are white already to harvest" (Jn. 4:35c).

The imagery of God is truly amazing, and I feel honored to share in it.

Tony Laidig
Artist

Table of Contents

Foreword

I first met Pastor Kelley Varner in 1987 while he was conducting a praise and worship seminar at Fort Bragg, North Carolina. The words that came forth during that meeting were spirit and life.

Proverbs 15:33 declares that "before honour is humility." Pastor Varner is a humble man, and God has honored him with wisdom, knowledge, and understanding. This man has taught me humility by example.

In the first chapter of Ephesians, Paul prayed that God would give His people the spirit of wisdom and revelation in the knowledge of Him, that the eyes of their understanding would be enlightened, and that they would know the hope of His calling (Eph. 1:17-18). I, too, have asked for these things, and God answered my prayer through Pastor Varner. I liken his ministry to that of Aquila and Priscilla, who taught Apollos "...the way of God more perfectly" (Acts 18:26). He has been that kind of teacher to me.

This message, "The Time of the Messiah," was birthed at our local church in a regional ministers' meeting during the 1995 Christmas season. That word is before you now in book form to help you see Jesus as rightful King and Lord, not just as the Babe in His nativity. It's time to allow the Spirit of the Son to grow up within us in order that the corporate Messiah, His glorious Church, may be His end-time witness to the world.

Pastor Elizabeth Gray
Johnsonville Deliverance Temple
Johnsonville, North Carolina

Preface

Judea, 4 B.C., 20 centuries ago...

Sanctified hope is whispering like a still, small voice in the hearts of devout Jews throughout the land. No clear prophetic voice has been heard for 400 years, yet the spirit of prophecy is fluttering afresh over the ancient writings of Isaiah and Micah like a great bird anticipating its descent.

Religious systems and would-be prophets are settled in their convictions as to the purpose and manner of Messiah's advent.

The injustice of worldly Roman oppression is crying out for vengeance. Poverty, ignorance, and disease continue to plunder the people.

Enquiring angels are assembling for choir practice.

Demons are snickering, ignorant and unchallenged.

Wicked King Herod is proud of his "politically correct" rebuilt temple.

The priestly house of Zacharias and Elisabeth is quiet.

A young couple from the house of David are laughing as they plan their wedding and their future together.

Somewhere in Jerusalem, an old man is still alive because God's unfulfilled promise is stronger than the last enemy.

In a small prayer chamber inside the house of the Lord, an old woman weeps and prays, as she has done for the past 80 years.

Gabriel is reminding Daniel of his famous prophecy.

Faithful shepherds, like David, are singing over their folds.

Wise men are scanning the heavens.

The heart of the sovereign God is stirring with the awareness of an everlasting, intertheistic covenant. The bosom of the Father is swelling with love, inspired to speak His Word.

The Holy Spirit, the power of the Highest, stands ready to overshadow a habitation of purity.

The stage is set. It's time for the Deliverer to appear.

Gal. 4:1-5, NIV

> *What I am saying is that as long as the heir is a child, he is no different from a slave, although he owns the whole estate.*
>
> *He is subject to guardians and trustees until the time set by his father.*
>
> *So also, when we were children, we were in slavery under the basic principles of the world.*
>
> *But when the time had fully come, God sent His Son, born of a woman, born under law,*
>
> *to redeem those under law, that we might receive the full rights of sons.*

1 Tim. 3:16, KJV

> *And without controversy great is the mystery of godliness: God was manifest in the flesh....*

1 Tim. 3:16, NIV

> *Beyond all question, the mystery of godliness is great: He appeared in a body....*

Jesus came! The Word was made flesh, and tabernacled among us (Jn. 1:14).

Jesus is coming!

Once again, it's time for the Messiah to appear! The purpose of His coming, then and now, is to redeem His people, to endow them with the spirit of sonship (Jn. 1:12; Rom. 8:14).

My previous book, *Whose Right It Is,* clearly explained that King Jesus will literally return to this planet. After historically and biblically examining the roots of classical Scofieldian dispensationalism, we learned that Jesus' "second" coming is not imminent, or "any minute." When examining its timing, the key word is *until* (see Ps. 110:1; Acts 3:19-21; Eph. 4:13; Jas. 5:7).

It was also established that Jesus' first coming is a "seed" form, a patterned picture of His second coming. The Son came forth from Mary's virgin womb in "the fullness of the time" (Gal. 4:4).

In this sequel to *Whose Right It Is,* four chapters of Scripture unfold the season of the Messiah's first appearing (Mt. 1–2; Lk. 1–2), showing the spiritual climate of His day to be:

1. A time of *wonder* (Mt. 1:18-25).

   The Messiah cannot be explained!

2. A time of *witness* (Lk. 1:1-80).

   The Messiah cannot be silenced!

3. A time of *warfare* (Mt. 2:13-23; Lk. 2:1-52).

   The Messiah cannot be contaminated!

4. A time of *worship* (Mt. 2:1-12).

   The Messiah cannot be dethroned!

The "desire of all nations" is Messiah, both Head and Body; that unique grammatical statement in Haggai 2:7 (with a singular subject and a plural verb) literally reads, "the desire of all nations, they shall come." It's the unveiling of the nature, majesty, and glory of the Pattern Son in a family of sons (Rom. 8:19). This describes the time for Christ to be fully formed in a people (Gal. 4:19; Col. 1:27)—His glorious Church, a many-membered new creation Man, the Body of Christ. The Latin word for "body" is *corpus*—there is a *corporate Messiah*!

Dan. 7:22, KJV

> *...judgment was given to the saints of the most High; and the time came that the saints possessed the kingdom.*

Throughout the Body of Christ, there is a fresh hunger and thirst for our foreordained destiny, an inspired expectation of what God is about to do in the earth. God's watchmen everywhere are prophesying, "This is the day of the Church. It's time to move on to the next level of God's ongoing purpose."

1 Chron. 12:32, KJV

> *And of the children of Issachar, which were men that had understanding of the times, to know what Israel ought to do....*

The Living Bible says that the men of Issachar "knew the best course for Israel to take," and Moffatt's translation adds that they "knew the needs of the time." The Jerusalem Bible says that they were "sound judges of the times when Israel should take action, and the way to do it."

Rom. 13:11, NIV

And do this, understanding the present time. The hour has come for you to wake up from your slumber, because our salvation is nearer now than when we first believed.

In God, timing is everything. Do you know what time it is?

Ps. 119:126, KJV

It is time for Thee, Lord, to work....

Ps. 102:13, KJV

Thou shalt arise, and have mercy upon Zion: for the time to favour her, yea, the set time, is come.

Journey with me back to 4 B.C. The King and His Kingdom were about to come. Heaven and earth, God and man, were about to mysteriously mingle in one holy Seed.

An understanding of the time of Messiah's first advent will arm and equip us to recognize and acknowledge the present season of the Holy Spirit upon the end-time Church. Let's take a fresh look at Matthew's and Luke's insightful accounts of the Christmas story—*The Time of the Messiah.*

Pastor Kelley Varner
Praise Tabernacle
Richlands, North Carolina

He's Not Just a Baby Anymore

During the Christmas season, most people easily relate to the Christchild because the infant Redeemer poses little threat to their way of living. But the Baby became a Man, and the Man Christ Jesus is now our Savior, Healer, Baptizer, King, and Judge.

My friend and colleague, Michael A. Smith, prophetic psalmist and pastor of Victory Fellowship, West Memphis, Arkansas, was given this song by the Lord: "He's Not Just a Baby Anymore..."

The prophets spoke of One to come, His name is Jesus,
To save His people from their sins, this was His purpose,
For unto us a Child is born, a Son is given,
To establish His own throne in Earth and Heaven.

As a Child, He came to Earth born of a virgin,
The Son of God from royal birth, God's revelation,
The promise now had become true, a King and Kingdom,
To rule and reign in all the earth is His dominion.

He's not just a Baby anymore,
He has grown up to become great Conqueror,
He is called Wonderful, Counsellor,
And He's not just a Baby anymore.

He is Messiah, Jehovah,
He is the King of kings,
The Holy One of Israel,
He is the Prince of peace,
He's the Lion of Judah,
The Lamb of God is He,
Your Redeemer, my Healer,
The One who made us free.

He's not just a Baby anymore,
He has grown up to become great Conqueror,
He is called Wonderful, Counsellor,
And He's not just a Baby anymore.

So worship Him, the Champion,
Delivered from the curse,
All creation sings, Hallelujahs ring
To the King of the universe.
So bow down before Him,
He sits upon the throne,
He lays not in a manger,
Won't you make your heart His home?

He is Messiah, Jehovah,
He is the King of kings,
The Holy One of Israel,
He is the Prince of peace.

But most of all, remember, please,
What all of this is for,
He's not just a Baby,
He's not a little Baby,
He's not just a Baby anymore![1]

---

1. Copyright 1986. Words and music by Michael A. Smith.

Chapter One

Christ, the Anointed Seed

"...unto Christ...."

Matthew 1:17

It's time for the Messiah!

"Messiah" is the Old Testament equivalent of the Greek word *Christos*, which was transliterated into the English "Christ." Both terms mean "the anointed one."

Jn. 4:25-26, KJV

> *The woman saith unto Him, I know that Messias cometh, which is called Christ: when He is come, He will tell us all things.*
>
> *Jesus saith unto her, I that speak unto thee am He.*

In the Old Testament, prophets (1 Kings 19:16), priests (Ex. 40:13-15), and kings (1 Sam. 16:1,13) were anointed, or consecrated with oil—set apart unto those offices.

Jesus is the Messiah, the Christ: He is Prophet (Acts 3:22-23), Priest (Heb. 7:26), and King (Rev. 19:16). But the

New Testament reveals "Christ" to be both Head and Body! Jesus is our glorious Head, and we are His Church, the Body of Christ—the *corporate Messiah*! This anointed, sanctified "royal priesthood" (1 Pet. 2:9) is a prophetic people who have been made kings and priests unto God (Rev. 1:6; 5:10).

Christ in You

1 Tim. 3:16, KJV

And without controversy great is the mystery of godliness: God was manifest in the flesh....

1 Tim. 3:16, NIV

Beyond all question, the mystery of godliness is great: He appeared in a body....

The apostle Paul unfolded this Messianic mystery in his Epistle to the Colossians.

Col. 1:25-27, NIV

I have become its servant by the commission God gave me to present to you the word of God in its fullness—

the mystery that has been kept hidden for ages and generations, but is now disclosed to the saints.

To them God has chosen to make known among the Gentiles the glorious riches of this mystery, which is Christ in you, the hope of glory.

The word *you* in Colossians 1:27 is a plural pronoun. The phrase literally reads, "Christ in and among all of you."

There are two extremes among Christians. First, there are those who only see Christ the Head. Some have never experienced the Holy Ghost in the Pentecostal dynamic. These have never spoken with other tongues or experienced the supernatural gifts of the Spirit.

The primary reason for the current "laughing revival" throughout the nations is to introduce the present reality of the power of God to folks who have never tasted it. Classical Pentecostals have been laughing in the Holy Ghost for almost a century. If you need to laugh, then laugh, for there will come a time when you will need to weep (Eccl. 3:4).

Hyper-dispensationalists, à la Darby, Scofield, and Larkin, have relegated apostles and prophets (Eph. 4:11) and the *charismata* (1 Cor. 12:8-10) solely to the Book of Acts. But these things happened only the day before yesterday (2 Pet. 3:8)! Calvary predicated Pentecost: first the blood, then the oil. Staunch evangelicals need to be introduced to the mystery of "Christ in you" (Col. 1:27) to perceive the Body of Christ by the Spirit.

Second, there are those who only emphasize the aforementioned mystery, Christ in His Body. The latter have stopped "holding the Head" (Col. 2:9); some have done away with His literal return to this planet. But I am not "Christ." You are not "Christ." Christ is not an individual; in His fullest expression, Christ is plural. He is the Anointed One of the New Testament—the Head and His Body, Jesus and His Church (1 Cor. 6:17). This corporate new creation is further explained by Paul in Ephesians to be the "new man" (Eph. 2:15; 4:24), "the inner man" (Eph. 3:16), and "a perfect man" (Eph. 4:13).

Furthermore, New Age metaphysics with its jacked-up, humanistic talk of a "Christ-consciousness" is certainly a devilish, bloodless counterfeit of Paul's revelation of "Christ in you," for it has nothing to do with Jesus' finished work and the subsequent outpouring of the Holy Ghost (Acts 2:33-36).

The real truth concerning the corporate "Christ" is that we His Church, His Body, collectively comprise the fullness of Him that fills all in all (Eph. 1:22-23). For that to happen corporately, He must be experienced personally. Paul reiterated this new creation reality in his Epistles to the Galatians and the Ephesians.

Gal. 4:6-7, NIV

Because you are sons, God sent the Spirit of His Son into our hearts, the Spirit who calls out, "Abba, Father."

So you are no longer a slave, but a son; and since you are a son, God has made you also an heir.

Eph. 5:18, KJV

...be filled with the Spirit.

Christ in you...the Spirit of the Son sent into our hearts...being filled with the Holy Ghost—these spiritual synonyms all express the same truth.

2 Cor. 4:4, KJV

...Christ, who is the image of God....

When Paul wrote to the church at Corinth, he defined "Christ" as "the image of God." The image of God, our future and destiny, is held within the Messianic seed! The pragmatic application and manifestation of Jesus' present reign is the Father's ultimate intention and expectation: a vast family of sons conformed to the image of the Firstborn, a corporate expression of Jesus' life and nature (Rom. 8:29; see also Gen. 1:26-28).

Ps. 22:22, NIV

I will declare Your name to my brothers; in the congregation I will praise You.

Is. 8:18, NIV

Here am I, and the children the Lord has given me. We are signs and symbols in Israel from the Lord Almighty, who dwells on Mount Zion.

Heb. 2:10-13, NIV

In bringing many sons to glory, it was fitting that God, for whom and through whom everything exists, should make the author of their salvation perfect through suffering.

Both the one who makes men holy and those who are made holy are of the same family. So Jesus is not ashamed to call them brothers.

He says, "I will declare Your name to My brothers; in the presence of the congregation I will sing Your praises."

And again, "I will put My trust in Him." And again He says, "Here am I, and the children God has given Me."

To accomplish this, the Father has sent forth the Spirit of His Son into our hearts. The spirit of Moses was multiplied and placed upon the 70 elders (Num. 11:24-25); even so, the New Testament Mediator has become a many-membered Man in His corporate Body!

Gal. 4:19, NIV

> *My dear children, for whom I am again in the pains of childbirth until Christ is formed in you.*

Gal. 4:19, TLB

> *...I am once again suffering for you the pains of a mother waiting for her child to be born—longing for the time when you will finally be filled with Christ.*

The mystery of this New Testament revelation began with a Seed planted in a habitation of purity, Mary's womb. Paul's apostolic, intercessory burden was that Christ, the Anointed One, the Spirit of the Son, be fully formed in a virgin Church! This glorious Body of Christ is the Church of the Firstborn, Mount Zion, the city of the living God (Heb. 12:22-23). Paul knew firsthand the reality of the indwelling Christ.

Gal. 1:15-16, KJV

> *But when it pleased God, who separated me from my mother's womb, and called me by His grace,*
>
> *To reveal His Son in me, that I might preach Him....*

It's time for the Messiah to appear; it's time for Christ to come. It's time for the Head of the Church to manifest Himself, to unveil Himself, to form Himself in a people, a Body—a corporate, many-membered Messiah. Chapter Nine of my book *Whose Right It Is* (pp. 235-240) clearly showed that the Lord will appear "in" the saints before He literally comes "with" the saints in the air. One primary feature of the Feast of Tabernacles (Jn. 7) is the appearing of the Lord.

Until Christ

Having established that "Messiah" is synonymous with "Christ," and that the term *Christ* in the New Testament applies to Jesus and His Body (constituting one new Man), we now examine the text before us, Matthew 1:1-17.

Mt. 1:1, KJV

> *The book of the generation of Jesus Christ, the son of David, the son of Abraham.*

In its consummate sense, the "book" of the generation of Jesus Christ is a people (2 Cor. 3:1-3)—"...the Lamb's book of life" (Rev. 21:27). Moffatt translates Matthew 1:1 as "the birth-roll of Jesus Christ." A Messianic people with His divine genes is "of the generation of Jesus Christ"; this mood is genitive, denoting origin and character.

"Generation" is singular—one spiritual generation in contrast with the many earthy "generations" of the first Adam (Gen. 5:1)—a heavenly people who have been produced from the character of the last Adam (1 Cor. 15:44-49), having been made partakers of the divine nature (2 Pet. 1:4). The word *generation* is commonly used with reference to time, but it essentially speaks about something being born and coming forth (with reference to nature).

The generation of Jesus Christ is a people who have been birthed out of Him! We are the "offspring" of God (Acts 17:29), His family. Adam was the federal head of a natural race. Jesus is the federal Head of a spiritual people who have been regenerated or born from above (Jn. 3:7).

Jesus Christ is the Seed of the woman (Gen. 3:15) as well as the Seed of Abraham and the Seed of David. Thus we see respectively His pain, His promise, and His power, as He relates to humanity racially (having become flesh), redemptively, and royally.

In that Seed is God's name or nature—all that God is, all that God has, and all that God does! The story of Bible history is "His story," the story of the Seed. In the volume of the Book, it is written of Him.

1. From Genesis to Malachi, the Seed comes (Gen. 3:15).
2. In the four Gospels, the Seed dies (Jn. 12:24).
3. In the Book of Acts, the Seed lives (Acts 2:24).
4. From Romans to Jude, the Seed speaks (Heb. 1:1).
5. In the Book of Revelation, the Seed reigns (Rev. 11:15).

Isaiah prophesied that Messiah would "see His seed" and that they would "prolong His days" (Is. 53:10). The story of the New Testament Church in the Book of Acts is the continuation of "...all that Jesus began both to do and teach" (Acts 1:1).

Mt. 1:16-17, KJV

And Jacob begat Joseph the husband of Mary, of whom was born Jesus, who is called Christ.

So all the generations from Abraham to David are fourteen generations; and from David until the carrying away into Babylon are fourteen generations; and from the carrying away into Babylon unto Christ are fourteen generations.

The legal Messianic genealogy of Matthew 1:1-17 contains a total of 42 generations.

From Abraham to David are 14 generations (Mt. 1:2-6a).

From David until the Babylonian captivity are 14 generations (Mt. 1: 6b-12a).

From the Babylonian captivity "unto Christ" are 14 generations (Mt. 1:12b-17).

However, in the latter section (Mt. 1:12b-17), there seems to be a contradiction. Jechonias was the 28th generation; following him are:

29. Salathiel.
30. Zorobabel.
31. Abiud.
32. Eliakim.
33. Azor.
34. Sadoc.
35. Achim.

36. Eliud.
37. Eleazar.
38. Matthan.
39. Jacob.
40. Joseph, the husband of Mary.
41. Jesus, who is called Christ.

Count them again. There seems to be a contradiction, a missing generation.

Where is the 42nd generation? Jesus had no earthly seed. Where is His generation? Who is the 42nd generation?

The answer is simple, found in the Greek phrase for "unto Christ" or "until Christ" in Matthew 1:17. This aligns with Paul's apostolic burden "until Christ be formed" in a people (Gal. 4:19), until the Messiah shows up in His anointed family.

The 42nd "generation" is the Church, the corporate Messiah, the Body of "Christ"! The Bible number denoting man is six. The number seven speaks of perfection. Forty-two is six times seven—the "perfect man" of First Corinthians 13:10-11 (where the key word is *when*), and Ephesians 4:13 (where the key word is *till*). The 42nd generation is a mature, many-membered Man, the corporate Messiah.

There is one family of God, one Body (Eph. 3:15; 4:4), and there is one Head of the Church (Eph. 1:22). One anointed Head (Jesus Christ) and one anointed Body (of Christ) equals one new Man—Christ, the Anointed One!

To reiterate, Christ, in the fullest sense, is not an individual...He is corporate. The secret of the anointing, the real power of the Holy Spirit, is to be found in His people; the new wine is in the cluster (Is. 65:8; Joel 3:18).

1 Cor. 6:17, KJV

But he that is joined unto the Lord is one spirit.

1 Jn. 4:17, KJV

...as He is, so are we in this world.

Who Shall Declare His Generation?

Jesus had no natural children. His seed is spiritual, a people begotten by the Word and Spirit of God (Jn. 3:1-8; Jas. 1:18; 1 Pet. 1:23). The first Adam is no longer our father. We are spirit beings of whom God Almighty is the Father (Heb. 12:9; see also Jas. 1:7).

The prophet Isaiah asked, "...and who shall declare His generation?" (Is. 53:8; Acts 8:33)

Ps. 22:30, KJV

A seed shall serve Him; it shall be accounted to the Lord for a generation.

Is. 53:10, KJV

...He shall see His seed, He shall prolong His days....

Jesus will realize the spiritual seed who shall prolong His days (Jn. 14:12; Acts 1:1). This enchristed seed (Gal. 3:16) is an anointed army of servants, the 42nd generation, the glorious, end-time Church marked by righteousness

(Ps. 14:5), prayer (Ps. 24:6), and praise (Ps. 102:18). Jesus is the true Vine and we are the branches extending out of Him (Jn. 15:1-5; see also Rom. 11:36).

1 Pet. 2:9-10, KJV

> *But ye are a chosen generation, a royal priesthood, an holy nation, a peculiar people; that ye should shew forth the praises of Him who hath called you out of darkness into His marvellous light:*
>
> *Which in time past were not a people, but are now the people of God: which had not obtained mercy, but now have obtained mercy.*

As to their interpretation of His first coming, political and religious leaders missed Messiah in His miraculous nativity. Men today, without the understanding of the Spirit, have set forth their own ideas in predicting His second coming.

Once again, it's time for Messiah to appear! It's time for the unveiling of the 42nd generation. It's time for the Anointed One to be fully fashioned in His people, His Church, His anointed seed.

The time of the Messiah is a time of faith, and faith is contrary to reason.

How did Messiah make His initial entrance?

First of all, that day was a time of *wonder*...

Chapter Two

A Time of Wonder

"...and His name shall be called Wonderful...."

Isaiah 9:6

The previous chapter established that the Old Testament word *Messiah* is equivalent to *Christ* and that the term *Christ* in the New Testament pertains to Jesus *and* His Body. The end-time Church, under the headship of Jesus Christ, is the corporate Messiah.

The next four chapters of this volume develop this foundational theme, showing that Messiah's season is:

1. A time of *wonder* (Mt. 1:18-25).

   The Messiah cannot be explained!

2. A time of *witness* (Lk. 1:1-80).

   The Messiah cannot be silenced!

3. A time of *warfare* (Mt. 2:13-23; Lk. 2:1-52).

   The Messiah cannot be contaminated!

4. A time of *worship* (Mt. 2:1-12).

   The Messiah cannot be dethroned!

First, the time of the Messiah is a time of inexplicable *wonder*! As noted, Paul described Jesus' incarnation as being a "mystery" or "sacred secret."

1 Tim. 3:16, KJV

And without controversy great is the mystery of godliness: God was manifest in the flesh….

A Virgin Shall Conceive

Is. 7:14, KJV

Therefore the Lord Himself shall give you a sign; Behold, a virgin shall conceive, and bear a son, and shall call His name Immanuel.

Mt. 1:18-25, NIV

This is how the birth of Jesus Christ came about: His mother Mary was pledged to be married to Joseph, but before they came together, she was found to be with child through the Holy Spirit.

Because Joseph her husband was a righteous man and did not want to expose her to public disgrace, he had in mind to divorce her quietly.

But after he had considered this, an angel of the Lord appeared to him in a dream and said, "Joseph son of David, do not be afraid to take Mary home as your wife, because what is conceived in her is from the Holy Spirit.

"She will give birth to a son, and you are to give Him the name Jesus, because He will save His people from their sins."

All this took place to fulfill what the Lord had said through the prophet:

"The virgin will be with child and will give birth to a son, and they will call Him Immanuel"—which means, "God with us."

When Joseph woke up, he did what the angel of the Lord had commanded him and took Mary home as his wife.

But he had no union with her until she gave birth to a son. And he gave Him the name Jesus.

Matthew's Gospel tells the story of Jesus' birth from the standpoint of Joseph, while Luke speaks from Mary's perspective.

Can you begin to imagine the conversation that took place between Joseph and his teenage fiancée when Mary first tried to describe Gabriel's visit?

"Joseph, I have something important to tell you!"

"What is it, my love?"

"I'm with child."

"What? Who got you pregnant?"

"The Holy Ghost..."

"Are you sure?"

"Yes."

"Who told you this? How could this happen? Tell me his name."

"Gabriel."

"I'll kill him!"

"You can't...he's an archangel; and he declared my pregnancy to be the fulfillment of prophetic Scripture."

The virgin birth of Jesus Christ really happened. Consider a similar episode 700 years before that, when the prophet Isaiah rushed home one afternoon to tell his wife the good news.

"Honey, I've heard from God!"

"That's terrific, dear. What did He say?"

"Jehovah said that a virgin would conceive, bear a son, and call His name, 'God with us'."

"You're not going to preach that, are you?"

The Lord waited seven centuries to vindicate the word of His servant, who went to his grave without seeing the fulfillment of his trailblazing prophecy (see Deut. 18:22). The night Jesus was born, Isaiah turned to the "multitude of the heavenly host" (Lk. 2:13) and said, "I told you so!" The incarnation absolutely took place (Jn. 1:14; Rom. 1:3-4; Heb. 2:14-17); it's happening again as a remnant Church, His ongoing incarnation, is being overshadowed by the same Holy Ghost.

The "holy thing" in Mary's womb was unprecedented (Lk. 1:35). He was the miraculous Bread from Heaven, typified in the Old Testament by the daily "manna," which means "What is it?" (Ex. 16 with Jn. 6). He was "very God" harmonized with "very Man"—Jesus, the divine synergism.

The time of the Messiah is a season when Heaven comes to earth, the invisible made visible. God's ways and thoughts are far above those of mere men (Is. 55:8-9). His intentions for us in Christ are exceeding abundantly above all we can ask or think (Eph. 3:20).

Born of God

God is going forth in the earth in ways that defy explanation. Revival is spontaneously breaking out as the

Church begins to "show" the evidence of His inward life. Like the virgin birth of Messiah, these things have never happened before. The Day of the Lord is dawning. The sovereign One is doing what He's always done: "whatsoever He hath pleased" (Ps. 115:3).

He is doing a "new thing" (Is. 43:19) in you and in your church...all by Himself.

This "new thing"—the anointed seed—is a "holy thing," wrought by the overshadowing ability of the Holy Ghost.

Lk. 1:35, KJV

And the angel answered and said unto her, The Holy Ghost shall come upon thee, and the power of the Highest shall overshadow thee: therefore also that holy thing which shall be born of thee shall be called the Son of God.

Incredibly, the *same* seed that was implanted in the virgin's womb was the living Word sown in the good ground of our hearts whereby we were born from above (Jn. 3:1-8)! This divine law or principle is first seen in Genesis 1:11-12 where we understand that everything reproduces after its own "kind," its own "sort or species." When you squeeze a real Christian, God comes out.

Jas. 1:18, KJV

Of His own will began He us with the word of truth, that we should be a kind of firstfruits of His creatures.

1 Pet. 1:23, KJV

Being born again, not of corruptible seed, but of incorruptible, by the word of God, which liveth and abideth for ever.

That *same* kind of seed, producing the "same image" (2 Cor. 3:18), is incorruptible or indestructible. Don't be nervous; it cannot decay. All hell may be breaking loose in the external, circumstantial, appearance realm; but the seed is okay. Lions can't eat it, water can't drown it, and fire can't burn it! We have been begotten again by the word of truth, or reality. You may look like a basket case, but there is something real going on inside! The hope we hold for ourselves and our children lies within the indwelling seed. The cream will rise.

1 Jn. 3:9, KJV

> *Whosoever is born of God....*

1 Jn. 5:4, KJV

> *For whatsoever is born of God....*

God is a spirit (Jn. 4:24)—and that which is born of God is brought forth by the Spirit. The New Testament reveals that *whosoever* or *whatsoever* (a ministry, a proposed marriage, a business, an idea) that has been birthed by the Spirit:

1. Is destined for Kingdom rulership (Mt. 2:2).
2. Is holy (Lk. 1:35).
3. Is not of man's will or flesh (Jn. 1:13).
4. Is from above (Jn. 3:5).
5. Is spirit (Jn. 3:6).
6. Is purposed to bear witness to the truth (Jn. 18:37).

7. Is incorruptible (indestructible) (1 Pet. 1:23).
8. Is righteous (1 Jn. 2:29).
9. Is love (godly, God-like) (1 Jn. 4:7).
10. Is powerful in faith to overcome the world (1 Jn. 5:4).

Prove all things with this tenfold spiritual litmus test. The fire that comes forth in the Day of the Lord will try every man's work of what sort it is (1 Cor. 3:12-15). The Feast Day of Atonement will bring everything into at-one-ment, or alignment. The plumbline with which He measures and adjusts all things is His Word, the divine seed (Amos 7:7-8). Only that which is truly born of God will stand.

Zech. 4:6, KJV

...Not by might, nor by power, but by My spirit, saith the Lord of hosts.

1 Cor. 4:20, NIV

For the kingdom of God is not a matter of talk but of power.

Phil. 2:13, KJV

For it is God which worketh in you both to will and to do of his good pleasure.

The Woman, Your Soul

The time of the Messiah is a time of *wonder*! Something (better yet, Someone) wonderful has been birthed within you that cannot be explained. Like Mary, you are carrying a holy Seed in your womb. Our time of growing in God (or His growing in us) is a time when we often wonder about days to come. Our future is locked up inside that divine Germ.

Man is a trichotomy—spirit, soul, and body (1 Thess. 5:23). "Salvation" (the Greek word is *soteria*) is a misnomer to most Christians, for "salvation" means "a complete deliverance" and encompasses far more than regeneration. This truth is explained in depth in Chapter Two of my book *Prevail: A Handbook for the Overcomer* (Shippensburg, PA: Destiny Image, 1982). There we learned that the new birth is the beginning of our salvation, and that salvation is progressive as well as once and for all. Your spirit has been saved, your soul is being saved, and your body shall be saved.

2 Cor. 1:10, KJV

> *Who delivered us from so great a death, and doth deliver: in whom we trust that He will yet deliver us.*

First, your spirit has been saved. When a man is born from above, his spirit is resurrected and passed from the death of trespasses and sins unto a brand-new life in Christ (Jn. 5:24; Eph. 2:1). His candle is lit by Jesus the Savior (Prov. 20:27; Jn. 1:9; 8:12), and he becomes a new creation (2 Cor. 5:17). In justification, he receives a new standing; in regeneration, a new heart.

Second, your soul is being saved. The transformation of the soul is the renewing (renovating) of the mind (Rom. 12:1-2) from strength to strength (Ps. 84:7), from faith to faith (Rom. 1:17), and from glory to glory (2 Cor. 3:18).

To live is to grow and to grow is to change—spiritual growth denotes change after change after change! This transformation is by the power of the Spirit, ministered by Jesus the Baptizer (Acts 1:5; 2:1-4). Grace is a progression (2 Pet. 3:18).

The apostle James instructed us to "receive with meekness the engrafted word, which is able to save your souls" (Jas. 1:21b). The New International Version mentions "the word planted in you." The word for "engrafted" is *emphutos* (#1721 in James Strong's *The Exhaustive Concordance of the Bible,* Peabody, MA: Hendrickson Publishers, n.d.), which means "implanted" or "rooted." It comes from two Greek words:

1. *en,* which means "in."
2. *phuo,* which means "to puff or blow, to swell up; to germinate or grow (sprout, produce)." *Phuo* is translated as "spring (up)" in the King James Version three times (Lk. 8:6,8; Heb. 12:15). The breath of the Spirit made Mary's belly swell with new life.

Third, your body shall be saved (see Rom. 8:23; Eph. 1:14; 4:30; Phil. 3:21). God's plan is to save the whole man: spirit, soul, and body.

In gender and principle, spirit (*pneuma*) is masculine and soul (*psyche*) is feminine. In this view, Joseph can represent man's spirit and Mary the soul. Jesus, the divine Seed in the womb of Mary, was the implanted Word.

Every thought (like seed) has its source in one of three spirits—God's, man's, or the devil's. Our soul or mind is like a woman's womb, wherein conception (of thoughts) takes place. When fiery darts assail us, we must not receive them or meditate on them. Faith comes by thinking upon the Word of God (Rom. 10:17). Fear comes by contemplating the voice of the devil. The birth canal for this fertilized seed is the mouth; our words—the baby—are the fruit of our lips (Prov. 18:21; Is. 57:19; Mt. 12:34).

Mary's womb was like "the womb of the morning" (Ps. 110:3), anointed to give birth to a "new thing" in a new day. You may feel barren, but God might be saving you for Himself! He wants to plant His own royal nature in you without the help of men. He's been waiting until the womb is ready—a virgin womb, undefiled by earthly seed, or carnal ideas and procedures.

To summarize these thoughts in the light of Matthew 1:18-25, one can liken Joseph to the realm of spirit and Mary to the soul (mind). God, all by Himself, put Himself in you! He is doing a sovereign work in this third feast as He "tabernacles" Himself in the hearts of men (Deut. 16:16; see also Rev. 21:3). That divine Seed, the living Word, has come into union with the pure minds of those who are hungry for God. The operation of His Spirit in a man's heart is sacrosanct, intimate, and most holy.

Simply put, God has done and is doing something wonderful inside the "woman" that men cannot explain! And He's doing it without man's help....

The same seed, the living Word, that came into union with Mary's womb now fills our minds and hearts. How sad that so many church-going sinners in America are trying to live the Christian life without a genuine experience of regeneration (the new birth).

Furthermore, it is vain for men and women to try to parrot the gospel of the Kingdom when they cannot relate to Jesus as Lord. Believers struggle for a formation of Christ within them when there has been no impartation of the Seed, the living Word.

But the Word is growing within a people all by itself; the Word of God is inexplicably working mightily within us as it did in Mary's womb (Jer. 13:23; Mt. 6:27,33; Col. 1:29).

To make his calling and election sure, each believer must know that he has been overshadowed by the Holy Ghost and impregnated with the living Word. When that happens, you may say, "This can't be God. It's not possible." Just rest and be thankful as the Seed grows up from within, as the Word works, lives, and forms Himself in you.

Mk. 4:26-29, KJV

And He said, So is the kingdom of God, as if a man should cast seed into the ground;

And should sleep, and rise night and day, and the seed should spring and grow up, he knoweth not how.

For the earth bringeth forth fruit of herself; first the blade, then the ear, after that the full corn in the ear.

But when the fruit is brought forth, immediately he putteth in the sickle, because the harvest is come.

The Woman, Your Church

The time of the Messiah is a time of *wonder*—He cannot be explained!

We have seen that God plants Himself in the hearts of individuals. A broader application of this present-day, ongoing incarnation likens Joseph to the "husbandman" ministries in the Body of Christ—the ones who carry the seed of His Word—the fivefold ministry, especially apostles and prophets (Eph. 2:20; 3:1-5; 4:11). The Greek word for "seed" is *sperma* (Strong's #4690), which means "something sown, seed (including the male 'sperm')." The Scriptures reveal these seed-carriers or "husbandmen" to be fathers and shepherds (see Gen. 9:20; Mt. 21:33-41; Jn. 15:1; 2 Tim. 2:6; Jas. 5:7).

Jer. 31:24, KJV

> *And there shall dwell in Judah itself, and in all the cities thereof together, husbandmen, and they that go forth with flocks.*

Paul likened the "woman" to the Church (Eph. 5:22-33). In Matthew 1:18-25, Mary can also depict the virgin Church, locally and universally.

Preachers today are nervous. Men who have run out of answers are frustrated. Something is happening in the midst of their ministries that cannot be interpreted. To those who are not secure in their calling, things seem to be out of hand, out of their control. What's a man to do? The Holy Spirit has overshadowed their "woman"—local assemblies are with child, without the help of man's flesh! This holy temple is being put together without the sound of the workman's hammer (1 Kings 6:7; Eph. 2:21-22).

In the 1960s and 1970s, the Holy Spirit was sovereignly poured out upon every denomination. He has begun to move that way again, with or without our permission. Moreover, the Holy Ghost is being poured out on the street, in barrooms, schools, prisons, and stadiums. Men have faked their way through the Feasts of Passover and Pentecost, but that which is within the veil, the realm of worship, must be real.

The average American Christian wants his freedom, a life of convenience—covenant with God on his own terms. But God, without explaining Himself, has touched us anew.

Ps. 127:1, KJV

Except the Lord build the house, they labour in vain that build it: except the Lord keep the city, the watchman waketh but in vain.

Don't Put Me Away!

Mt. 1:18-19, KJV

Now the birth of Jesus Christ was on this wise: When as His mother Mary was espoused to Joseph, before they came together, she was found with child of the Holy Ghost.

Then Joseph her husband, being a just man, and not willing to make her a publick example, was minded to put her away privily.

Mary was "espoused" or "engaged to be married" to Joseph. Espousal was commonly an interval of 10 to 12 months, and the betrothed maiden remained with her own family. This "just" or "righteous" man (Mt. 1:19; Lk. 1:6) had wooed and won her. Like the Ark of the

Covenant that was covered with gold on the inside and the outside, Mary was beautiful, for God Himself had been attracted to her!

Joseph was observant of custom and rule in his dutiful obligations to God and men. It is my opinion that he, too, was a virgin. Sometimes crazy things happen to crazy people who do crazy things, but Joseph was straight, walking upright before the Lord. He had sanctified and reserved their physical union until marriage, for it was the right thing to do. Joseph was no wimp. He was a businessman, a carpenter, in good shape physically and financially—right things.

Heb. 13:4, NIV

> *Marriage should be honored by all, and the marriage bed kept pure, for God will judge the adulterer and all the sexually immoral.*

Upon hearing Mary's incredible announcement, this righteous man probably thought, "My life is over." But Joseph was not "willing" or "desirous" to exhibit or display Mary to any kind of open shame. The legal penalty for adultery (even in espousal) was death (Deut. 22:21-24; Jn. 8:4-5). The bewildered beau was thus "minded" or "willing" to put her away privately, unnoticed. The word for "put away" in Matthew 1:19 is *apoluo* (Strong's #630) and means "to free fully, (literally) relieve, release, dismiss (reflexively, depart), or (figuratively) let die, pardon (or specially) divorce." In those times, the covenantal relationship of espousal could only be broken by "divorce." Joseph was willing to set her free, to let her go (Mt. 5:31-32; 19:7). But suspected virtue can afford to wait.

Every born-again, Spirit-filled Christian has been impregnated with the Seed of God. Each can say, "I have been overshadowed by the Holy Ghost. Yet I cannot fully explain what is happening within me. Don't be ashamed of me because the life of God is within me. Please don't put me away!"

Men want to tag and stereotype you, to press you into their own religious mold. If you don't fit their style, they'll take your credentials and give you the left foot of fellowship! But this new and holy thing cannot be labeled or explained.

Local churches everywhere are being caressed by the sovereign power of the Highest. The ministry of mere men has had little if anything to do with it. The commandment of the Lord is clear to every disconcerted pastor: Stay with your woman. Don't abandon the local church to preserve your own ministry when the unexplainable happens. Don't be ashamed of what the Holy Ghost has done; don't shun apostolic ministries who carry the Seed of God (see Mt. 13:38; Rom. 1:16; 2 Tim. 1:8,12,16). The Word is growing, and we are showing!

As with Joseph, it will cost you to relate with those who are pregnant with the holy Seed. A man or woman full of God is someone to deal with. Covenantal commitment is foundational in the time of the Messiah. We must add our faith to one another and mingle it with God's, believing that His Word will come to pass. Are we going to put each other away, or are we going to have this divine baby?

Rom. 5:5, KJV

And hope maketh not ashamed; because the love of God is shed abroad in our hearts by the Holy Ghost which is given unto us.

Fearful men have built ministries without the help of the Lord. In the words of the apostle, they have run "in vain" (Gal. 2:2; Phil. 2:16). Human wisdom and strength have attempted to push the power of the Holy Spirit down the steps of the church basement on Sunday night (Acts 26:26). Strategies have come and gone, void of resurrection life (Rom. 8:11). Don't be afraid, Joseph. Don't get "run" in your feet. Ultimately, the divine Wonder will "save much people alive" (Gen. 50:20).

Mt. 1:20, KJV

But while he thought on these things, behold, the angel of the Lord appeared unto him in a dream, saying, Joseph, thou son of David, fear not to take unto thee Mary thy wife: for that which is conceived in her is of the Holy Ghost.

"Now while he had this in his mind..." is the literal Greek rendering of Matthew 1:20.

In the time of the Messiah, things seem illogical. There are no easy answers, no quick fixes!

Sometimes we pray and hear nothing from God. Joseph may have inquired, "Where are You, Lord? I'm a just man. I've kept my covenantal relationship with Mary pure in accordance with Your Word, and I don't understand what has happened...she wouldn't lie to me.

We're embarrassed to talk to any of our family or friends (not to mention the priest down at the local synagogue) about these things—they would deem us mad. Lord, I just wanted to have a normal marriage, an ordinary life, and work my business. Our plans are ruined. Mary and I had the date set and the invitations have been sent. Why has all this happened to me?"

Joseph wasn't ready to be an earthly daddy to an eternal Spirit. Mary hadn't been trained to change God's diapers or teach Him how to walk. They weren't prepared to raise God. You won't learn the mystery of godliness—God manifested in the flesh (1 Tim. 3:16)—in any Bible school. There is no class to learn this stuff in. Until others have been visited by the apostolic angel and impregnated with the same Seed, they cannot hear your heart. That's why we feel closer to the members of His family, those who do His will, than to our own flesh and blood (Mt. 12:46-50)! The bond of the Spirit is greater than the bond of the flesh (Eph. 4:3).

Somebody says, "But, Pastor Varner, I need answers." What would you do with them if you had them? There is the mystery of iniquity (2 Thess. 2:3-4) and the mystery of godliness. Man has yet to discover how vile he is by himself or how great he can become in God. No one save the Pattern Son has plumbed the depths or the heights of those questions; He alone descended to the lowest parts of the earth to put away our sins, then was exalted above the highest heaven (Eph. 4:8-10).

"But while he thought on these things..." (Mt. 1:20). Sometimes we think too much. I have upset the people I pastor and the preachers I relate to by answering their inquiries with three little words: "I don't know." Men want to know all the answers so they can control God and other people. But the Almighty has put us in the middle of something that we can't explain, and has made it so good that we don't want to get out of it! Heaven and earth have kissed each other, and we have been caught in the middle of the "smack."

Joseph did not act from impulse. Because of his great love for Mary, he couldn't talk about Gabriel's visit with his friends. They wouldn't believe something he couldn't explain. So the righteous carpenter paused in the use of reason, sought for the right course, and God came to his help. It is not enough to just follow Providence; we must inquire in His temple (Ps. 27:4).

If we will wait upon the Lord, the same angel, the same message, will come and deliver us from fear. Joseph was admonished to "take Mary to his side," for this new and holy thing in the virgin's womb was begotten of God, kin to the Holy Ghost. This kingly seed, the fulfillment of the prophetic Scriptures, had been sent to deliver.

Matthew 1:20 also reveals that Joseph was a "son of David." This entire contextual setting has to do with the Kingdom of God. Because God is sovereign, the angel can say, "Fear not." This phrase is mentioned 365 times in the Bible—once for every day of the year. No one among us is completely fearless. But we have been fertilized with the divine Seed.

2 Tim. 1:7, KJV

For God hath not given us the spirit of fear; but of power, and of love, and of a sound mind.

"...Mary thy wife..." (Mt. 1:20)—this phrase could also represent the gifts or graces, the ministry, that God has given. Our "Mary" could be a business or an idea. She's still yours, Joseph! Too many think, "I'm just going to let God do it." No! Every miracle in the Bible required a cooperation between God and man. We are laborers together with Him. The difference, Joseph, is that the Holy Ghost is involved now! Mary is full of God. The Seed was "in" her, not "of" her.

Mt. 1:21, KJV

And she shall bring forth a son, and thou shalt call His name JESUS: for He shall save His people from their sins.

"Jesus" means "Jehovah our salvation." The Messianic purpose is salvific. His name is salvation because He shall save "His" people—not just a people—from their sins, especially the sin of unbelief (Jn. 16:8). We are not completely convinced that God meant what He said. The first thing He must do in the time of the corporate Messiah is permeate the Church with Himself with the intent to fully cleanse His people.

Mt. 1:22-25, KJV

Now all this was done, that it might be fulfilled which was spoken of the Lord by the prophet, saying,

Behold, a virgin shall be with child, and shall bring forth a son, and they shall call His name Emmanuel, which being interpreted is, God with us.

Then Joseph being raised from sleep did as the angel of the Lord had bidden him, and took unto him his wife:

And knew her not till she had brought forth her first-born son: and he called His name JESUS.

Matthew 1:22-23 fulfills Isaiah 7:14, uttered over 700 years before Messiah was born. In the Greek text, verse 23 has the definite article—"the" virgin. The virgin birth of Jesus Christ (Lk. 1:34; Heb. 10:5) is foundational to our faith. His body was prepared pure and holy, free from the corruption of sin. He thus qualified as Heaven's sinless, spotless Lamb, offered in pure sacrifice to God for the sins of the world (Jn. 1:29; Heb. 9:24-28).

We are being raised by revelation, fully awakened to recognize "Emmanuel," and know that "God is with us." This mystery needs to be "interpreted" or "explained" (Mt. 1:23)—thus the purpose of this writing. The apostolic angel aroused Joseph from the sleep of unbelief (Mt. 1:24; see also Acts 12:7; Eph. 5:14), and he "took" Mary as his wife. This word is *paralambano* (Strong's #3880) and means "to receive near, associate with oneself (in any familiar or intimate act or relation); by analogy, to assume an office; figuratively, to learn."

Joseph "knew" her not until Messiah was born. This verb in Matthew 1:25 is imperfect, denoting continuous action in the past. Joseph lived in continence with Mary until the birth of Jesus, her firstborn Son; she would later have other children (Mt. 12:46; 13:55).

Jesus is the "firstborn" or "firstbegotten" Son (see Lk. 2:7; Rom. 8:29; Col. 1:15,18; Heb. 1:6; Rev. 1:5). The anointed Body of Christ is the Church of the "firstborn" (Heb. 12:23).

The name of "Jesus"—the name above every name (Acts 4:12; Phil. 2:9-11; Heb. 1:4)—was given Him at the time of His circumcision by Joseph according to the angel's instructions (Lk. 2:21).

The removal of humanity's mental anguish comes with the revelation of God's redemptive plan. Joseph discovered three things about Jesus: His birth was supernatural, His mission was remedial, and His nature was divine.

Now, as then, the time of the unveiling of the Messiah is a time of unexplained *wonder*! God did not consult Joseph or Mary, nor did He ask their permission when He invaded their private world. What a strange way to bring salvation to men! Joseph's reputation would be ruined for years to come (Mt. 13:55; Lk. 4:22). Having a son meant everything in that day. In order to be tempted in all points like as we are, Jesus would have to receive the unjust accusation of being illegitimate (Heb. 4:15).

This new thing must be birthed in the hearts of men by the revelation of the Spirit (Is. 43:18-19), not by human might or power (Zech. 4:6). What God has done of and by the Holy Ghost will bring great deliverance. This move of God is not a Baptist thing, a Pentecostal thing, or a Kingdom thing—it's a holy thing!

Look back over your life for the past 15 years...10 years...5 years. Has everything happened as you expected? Have you had any surprises—circumstances for which you had no answers? The time of the Messiah is a time of wonder. These are tough times for men who walk by sight and not by faith, who are trying to interpret these days in view of their preconceived ideas.

Messiah cannot be explained. Now the *wonder* becomes a *witness*—once the Seed has been planted in a virgin womb, once the new thing has been birthed in you by His Spirit, He must speak...

Chapter Three

A Time of Witness

"He...was sent to bear witness of that Light."

John 1:18

It's time for the Messiah!

The first chapter of Matthew's Gospel revealed His first glorious Advent season to be a time of *wonder*—He cannot be explained. Now we turn to the beginning of Luke's Messianic narrative (Lk. 1:1-80), energized with the spirit of prophecy. The time of wonder becomes a time of *witness*—Messiah cannot be silenced!

That divine Baby lying in the manger pictures the infantile corporate Messiah, a prophetic people. The world is clamoring for someone to arise who really knows what he is talking about. The God who answers by fire is God (1 Kings 18:24). The corporate Messiah now speaking is comprised of men and women who are flames of fire (Heb. 1:7).

God is doing a new and holy thing in our hearts and ministries (Lk. 1:35). Like Mary, we have been overshadowed by the Holy Ghost and imbued with divine Seed.

We are not perfect, but the seed of perfection has been birthed in our hearts. Something wonderful has happened to us. We have been born again and filled with His Spirit! Paul explained this mystery to the Ephesians and Colossians.

Eph. 3:17-20, KJV

That Christ may dwell in your hearts by faith; that ye, being rooted and grounded in love,

May be able to comprehend with all saints what is the breadth, and length, and depth, and height;

And to know the love of Christ, which passeth knowledge, that ye might be filled with all the fulness of God.

Now unto Him that is able to do exceeding abundantly above all that we ask or think, according to the power that worketh in us.

Col. 1:27-29, NIV

To them God has chosen to make known among the Gentiles the glorious riches of this mystery, which is Christ in you, the hope of glory.

We proclaim Him, admonishing and teaching everyone with all wisdom, so that we may present everyone perfect in Christ.

To this end I labor, struggling with all His energy, which so powerfully works in me.

This new thing was birthed by revelation—"Christ in you" is wonderful (Col. 1:27). The seed of the living Word in you must prophesy. Someone says, "I can't speak; I'm just naturally nervous. " To that I reply, "Which nature?" Each of us can vocalize the divine nature (1 Cor. 14:1,5,24,31,39)!

Ps. 107:2, KJV

Let the redeemed of the Lord say so....

Rev. 19:10, KJV

...for the testimony of Jesus is the spirit of prophecy.

By the spirit of prophecy, believers can say things that natural men cannot say. How tragic that many evangelical, born-again Christians, shortchanged by religious tradition, have been told that the *charismata*, the gifts of the Holy Spirit (1 Cor. 12:8-10), particularly the gift of prophecy, are not for us today.

But the very *nature* of the Seed who saved us must speak! The virgin Mary was filled with the Word made flesh, the spirit of prophecy. John leaped, but Jesus talked and sang! Mary's Magnificat (Lk. 1:46-55) was the song of the "Chief Singer " (Hab. 3:19), the Lord Himself. Are you singing? In our corporate gatherings, the dove of the Holy Ghost flies around looking for someone to land on; if He lights upon you, you will sing!

In the time of the Messiah, the divine Seed within the true Church is speaking, singing, and praying! Part of our dilemma is that we cannot explain the thing we must tell. We're talking, talking, talking, but we sometimes don't know what we're talking about.

Do you remember when you were first saved? Did you tell it? Could you explain it? All you knew was that once you were blind, but now you could see (Jn. 9:25)!

Do you recall the birth of your first child? Did you make any phone calls? Were you ashamed or afraid to share that good news with others? You who are saved have been impregnated with the seed of God. Those who are Abraham's seed (Gal. 3:29) have nations within them (Gen. 12:1-3). The Seed you are carrying contains your future. In Christ, you are worth reproducing. Don't withhold your witness in the time of the Messiah. Jesus spoke with great authority (Mt. 7:28-29). So can we in His name.

Chapter 1 of Luke's Gospel is filled with the declared Word of the Lord—the seed becomes a song (Is. 54:1-5):

1. John the Baptist was conceived (Lk. 1:1-25).
2. Ruling angels spoke the good news (Lk. 1:26-38).
3. Elisabeth prophesied (Lk. 1:39-45).
4. Mary sang the Song of the Lord (Lk. 1:46-56).
5. Zacharias prophesied (Lk. 1:57-80).

The introduction to Luke 1 sets forth the good doctor's purpose as he addresses "Theophilus," which means "friend of God" or "lover of God."

Lk. 1:1-4, KJV

Forasmuch as many have taken in hand to set forth in order a declaration of those things which are most surely believed among us,

Even as they delivered them unto us, which from the beginning were eyewitnesses, and ministers of the word;

It seemed good to me also, having had perfect understanding of all things from the very first, to write unto thee in order, most excellent Theophilus,

That thou mightest know the certainty of those things, wherein thou hast been instructed.

First, there must be a "declaration" or "recital" of the gospel.

Second, this must be done by those who are "eyewitnesses," those who have seen these things with their own eyes (Eph. 1:18).

Third, this narrative must be declared with "exact" and "accurate" understanding (2 Tim. 2:7; 1 Jn. 5:20).

Finally, the underlying purpose of this witness is that men might know the "certainty" or "security" of these things (Prov. 22:20-21).

The Witness of the Light

Jn. 1:6-7, KJV

There was a man sent from God, whose name was John.

The same came for a witness, to bear witness of the Light, that all men through him might believe.

Jn. 1:15, KJV

John bare witness of Him....

The time of the Messiah is a time of *witness*. John the Baptist, who came in the spirit of the prophet Elijah, was the anointed forerunner of Jesus Christ (Is. 40:1-5; Mal. 4:5-6). There is a present prophetic "Elijah" ministry in these days of the unveiling of the corporate Messiah. Jesus said that Elijah *had come* in the person of John (Mt. 17:12-13), and that Elijah *would come* and restore all things (Mt. 17:11; see also Acts 3:19-21). For a fuller treatment of this Elijah-Elisha ministry that precedes the manifestation of the corporate Son in the endtimes, see my notes on *Principles of Present Truth from First Kings, Second Kings, and Second Chronicles* (Richlands, North Carolina: Tabernacle Press, 1984).

Lk. 1:5-7, KJV

> *There was in the days of Herod, the king of Judaea, a certain priest named Zacharias, of the course of Abia: and his wife was of the daughters of Aaron, and her name was Elisabeth.*
>
> *And they were both righteous before God, walking in all the commandments and ordinances of the Lord blameless.*
>
> *And they had no child, because that Elisabeth was barren, and they both were now well stricken in years.*

Like Ezekiel, who was a priest before he became a prophet, so John the Baptist had a priestly background. His father was the priest Zacharias, whose name means "Jehovah has remembered." Zacharias was of the "course" or "daily service" of Abia, the eighth of the 24 Davidic orders of priests (1 Chron. 24:10; see also 2 Chron. 8:14). Eight is the Bible number that denotes a *new beginning*! Each of these courses did duty for eight days, from sabbath to sabbath, twice a year. At the Feast of Tabernacles, all 24 courses were present. "Abia" or

"Abijah" means "father (worshiper) of Jah." It has been calculated that Zacharias' course officiated April 7-13 and October 3-9.

The name of Zacharias' wife was Elisabeth, which means "God of the oath." The God of Abraham, Isaac, and Jacob was about to remember His covenant. She was a descendant of the priestly Aaron. In modern terms, Zacharias was a preacher married to a preacher's daughter.

The "commandments" refer to the moral law; the "ordinances" to the ritual law (Lk. 1:6). With regard to both, this righteous couple was "blameless" or "irreproachable." The seeming inexplicable fruit of their faithfulness was Elisabeth's barren womb. Having given up hope of producing any sons of promise, both were "well stricken" or "advanced" in years.

Lk. 1:8-12, KJV

And it came to pass, that while he executed the priest's office before God in the order of his course,

According to the custom of the priest's office, his lot was to burn incense when he went into the temple of the Lord.

And the whole multitude of the people were praying without at the time of incense.

And there appeared unto him an angel of the Lord standing on the right side of the altar of incense.

And when Zacharias saw him, he was troubled, and fear fell upon him.

Zacharias had obtained the lot of burning incense on the golden altar in the "temple," the *naos*, the "inner sanctuary" of the Lord; this was a once-in-a-lifetime experience for a priest! In this momentous event of Zacharias' life, God was about to interrupt man's schedule. The glory in Moses' face had faded long ago (2 Cor. 3:6-18; 4:6). The Levitical order was about to be changed (Heb. 7:12).

All this happened during the "time of incense," the time of prayer (Lk. 1:10; see also Ps. 141:2; Rev. 5:8; 8:3-4). The witness of the Light was birthed and bathed in prayer before he ever moved about in the watery womb of his aged mother.

Zacharias was performing his priestly functions before God when something happened that he could not explain. Indeed, it would "trouble" or "stir" him (Lk. 1:12). The New International Version says that he was "startled and was gripped with fear."

As Zacharias entered the holy place from the east, the archangel Gabriel (Lk. 1:19) appeared on the "north side" by the table of showbread (Ex. 26:35). After four centuries of hungry silence, men were ready to taste the Bread from Heaven (Jn. 6:32-35). The tribe of Dan (which means "judge") camped on the "north side" (Num. 2:25)—Zion's Judge and King was about to come (see Ps. 48:2; Is. 14:13; Ezek. 1:4; Jn. 5:22).

The archangel stood on the "right side" of the altar of incense (Lk. 1:11). This word, also translated as "right hand" in the King James Version, speaks of a place of honor, power, and authority, and it reveals:

1. The honor that Zacharias and Elisabeth were about to receive as the parents of John the Baptist.

2. The honor that John would receive as the preceding witness to His divine Cousin (Mt. 11:10-11).
3. The "right hand" of the Father to which Jesus the Word would be exalted as the true Altar of Incense—our Advocate and Intercessor (see Acts 2:33-36; Rom. 8:34; Eph. 1:20; 1 Pet. 3:22).

Lk. 1:13-17, KJV

But the angel said unto him, Fear not, Zacharias: for thy prayer is heard; and thy wife Elisabeth shall bear thee a son, and thou shalt call his name John.

And thou shalt have joy and gladness; and many shall rejoice at his birth.

For he shall be great in the sight of the Lord, and shall drink neither wine nor strong drink; and he shall be filled with the Holy Ghost, even from his mother's womb.

And many of the children of Israel shall he turn to the Lord their God.

And he shall go before Him in the spirit and power of Elias, to turn the hearts of the fathers to the children, and the disobedient to the wisdom of the just; to make ready a people prepared for the Lord.

These verses tell us much about the prophet John, whose name means "Jehovah is a gracious Giver, gift of God." They provide insight into the kind of prophetic ministry operating in these days of the corporate Messiah.

1. John was an answer to prayer (Jas. 5:16).
2. He was named or natured by God (Lk. 1:13).

3. His name revealed the grace of God (Jn. 1:17).
4. He would produce much joy (Rom. 14:17).
5. He would be great before the Lord (Gen. 12:2).
6. He would be a sanctified Nazarite (Num. 6:1-8), like Samson and Samuel (Judg. 13:4-5; 1 Sam. 1:11).
7. He would be filled with the Holy Ghost (Eph. 5:18).
8. He would "turn" or "convert" many to God (Acts 26:18).
9. He would fulfill Isaiah 40:1-5 and Malachi 4:5-6.

John's mission and message was to make ready a people "prepared," or "equipped, established, built," for the Lord (Lk. 1:17; see also Heb. 3:3-4; 11:7; 1 Pet. 3:20).

Lk. 1:18-25, KJV

And Zacharias said unto the angel, Whereby shall I know this? for I am an old man, and my wife well stricken in years.

And the angel answering said unto him, I am Gabriel, that stand in the presence of God; and am sent to speak unto thee, and to shew thee these glad tidings.

And, behold, thou shalt be dumb, and not able to speak, until the day that these things shall be performed, because thou believest not my words, which shall be fulfilled in their season.

And the people waited for Zacharias, and marvelled that he tarried so long in the temple.

And when he came out, he could not speak unto them: and they perceived that he had seen a vision in the temple: for he beckoned unto them, and remained speechless.

And it came to pass, that, as soon as the days of his ministration were accomplished, he departed to his own house.

And after those days his wife Elisabeth conceived, and hid herself five months, saying,

Thus hath the Lord dealt with me in the days wherein He looked on me, to take away my reproach among men.

Like Naomi in the Book of Ruth, this aged priest made the excuse that his day was over (Ruth 1:12). Zacharias had many questions, doubting Gabriel's glad tidings (Jas. 1:8). The word for "sent" in Luke 1:19 is *apostello,* which means "to send forth on a mission" with authority (compare Heb. 1:7,14). Because of his unbelief concerning this apostolic word (Jn. 16:8-9; Heb. 3:16-19), Zacharias became "dumb" or "silent" throughout Elisabeth's pregnancy. He would not be able to speak. The word rendered "speechless" in Luke 1:22 signifies that the priest became deaf and dumb. The only thing that can mute the witness of the Messiah is the aggravation of unbelief!

In the day of the corporate Messiah, ministries that refuse to believe the words of the apostolic angel will become spiritually speechless. Because they have not heard from God, they will have nothing to say. Cherished, man-made traditions mean more to them than the revealed Word of God (Mt. 15:9; Mk. 7:13; see also 1 Cor. 12:2).

Many have confessed unbelief at the *wonder* of the corporate Messiah, and the heavens have become brass; faithless men have come into the presence of a Priest who will not answer them (see Prov. 1:28; Song 5:6; Mic. 3:7; Jn. 19:9; Heb. 3:1).

The expectant multitude could not understand what had happened to Zacharias as he beckoned and nodded to them. When his weekly ministerial course was finished, the elderly priest went home and obeyed the Lord. Faith without works is dead (Jas. 2:17), and faith without words is dead.

Elisabeth conceived because she received the seed of Gabriel's announcement, and rejoiced that God had removed her "reproach" or "disgrace, defamation" (Lk. 1:25; see also 1 Sam. 1:6-10). She "hid" herself completely for five months (Lk. 1:24).

The *wonder* was about to become a *witness*! The "messenger" who would prepare the way of the Lord was now an embryonic reality (Mal. 3:1).

Ruling Angels Are Speaking

The keynote speaker of this next section (Lk. 1:26-38) is the archangel Gabriel.

"Archangel" (1 Thess. 4:16; Jude 9) is from the Greek *archaggelos*, which means "a chief angel." It is taken from two words:

1. *archo,* which means "to be first (in political rank or power)."
2. *aggelos,* which means "a messenger; a pastor."

The name "Gabriel" (Dan. 8:16; 9:21) means "mighty man of God, hero of God." It is taken from a Hebrew word meaning "a valiant man or warrior"; its root means "to be strong, to prevail."

Gabriel was a *ruling angel,* a Kingdom messenger. His ministry was marked by authority. As such, he can represent the ministry of the *apostles* in these times of the corporate Messiah. As with verse 19, the verb "send" in Luke 1:26 is *apostello;* it describes one sent forth or commissioned, fully authorized to represent the name of the one who sent him. Paul confirmed this truth in his letter to the Galatians (consider also 2 Thess. 1:7; 1 Tim. 5:21; Heb. 1:7; 12:22; 13:2; Rev. 1:20).

Gal. 4:14, KJV

> *And my temptation which was in my flesh ye despised not, nor rejected; but received me as an angel of God, even as Christ Jesus.*

Gal. 4:14, NIV

> *Even though my illness was a trial to you, you did not treat me with contempt or scorn. Instead, you welcomed me as if I were an angel of God, as if I were Christ Jesus Himself.*

Gabriel came in the sixth month to announce the birth of the Last Adam (1 Cor. 15:45); Adam, made in the image of God and given dominion, was created on the sixth day (Gen. 1:26-31). The Body of Christ is about to be impacted by the voice of the archangel, the apostolic company (Acts 13:13; 15:22; 21:8).

Lk. 1:26-29, KJV

> *And in the sixth month the angel Gabriel was sent from God unto a city of Galilee, named Nazareth,*
>
> *To a virgin espoused to a man whose name was Joseph, of the house of David; and the virgin's name was Mary.*
>
> *And the angel came in unto her, and said, Hail, thou that art highly favoured, the Lord is with thee: blessed art thou among women.*
>
> *And when she saw him, she was troubled at his saying, and cast in her mind what manner of salutation this should be.*

Gabriel was "sent" (*apostello,* as in Luke 1:19) to Nazareth, which means "branch," the dry ground where Jesus would grow up before the Father as a "tender plant" (Is. 53:2).

Mary pictures the *virgin Church,* individually and collectively—a habitation of purity. "Mary," like "Miriam," is taken from the Hebrew root *marah,* which means "to be bitter." Her name prophesies the pain of bringing forth the divine Seed, the Word of God (Ps. 48:6; Is. 21:3). Paul used the same language to convey his apostolic burden (Gal. 4:19; see also Rom. 8:22).

Gabriel "came in" or "entered" Mary's dwelling with the good news (Lk. 1:28). The mother of the Son of God was highly favored or graced *among,* not above, women (although the best texts or earliest manuscripts omit the phrase, "blessed art thou among women"). The archangel explained that she was "blessed" or "eulogized, praised." Gabriel did not worship Mary; he congratulated her.

Mary was "troubled" at this greeting (Lk. 1:29). The Greek word here is *diatarasso* and means "to disturb wholly, agitate (with alarm)." She was both upset and puzzled, and "cast in her mind," or "began to reason." This Greek word in Luke 1:29 is *dialogizomai* (Strong's #1260) and means "to reckon thoroughly, to deliberate (by reflection or discussion)"—to "reason through" (Mt. 16:7-8; Mk. 2:6-8; Lk. 3:15). Compare the English word *dialogue*.

The initial response to the apostolic company in the days of the corporate Messiah will cause an uproar throughout the Christian world. Men are wondering even now over the "manner" of this "salutation" or "greeting (by person or letter)." They aren't focused on what He will say; they are worried about what He *might* say! The word for "manner" in Luke 1:29 is *potapos* and means "from what country?" or "of what sort?" (Mt. 8:27)

Lk. 1:30-36, KJV

And the angel said unto her, Fear not, Mary: for thou hast found favour with God.

And, behold, thou shalt conceive in thy womb, and bring forth a son, and shalt call His name JESUS.

He shall be great, and shall be called the Son of the Highest: and the Lord God shall give unto Him the throne of His father David:

> *And He shall reign over the house of Jacob for ever; and of His kingdom there shall be no end.*
>
> *Then said Mary unto the angel, How shall this be, seeing I know not a man?*
>
> *And the angel answered and said unto her, The Holy Ghost shall come upon thee, and the power of the Highest shall overshadow thee: therefore also that holy thing which shall be born of thee shall be called the Son of God.*
>
> *And, behold, thy cousin Elisabeth, she hath also conceived a son in her old age: and this is the sixth month with her, who was called barren.*

The same archangel who prophesied Messiah's death on the cross (Dan. 9:20-27) now arrives over 450 years later to announce His virgin birth!

Mary was shaken up by Gabriel's initial appearance and greeting. She had yet to hear the "reason for the season." Gabriel explained that the virgin had obtained "favour" or "grace" with God. By that grace (2 Cor. 12:9) she would conceive in her womb a "son"—the Greek word *huios*, which means "a mature son." (For a fuller significance of these truths in Luke 1:31, review the previous chapter.)

The name of Mary's Son and the nature of that which is born of God is "Jesus"—"Jehovah is salvation" (Mt. 1:21)! He would inaugurate a new kind of faith (Heb. 12:1-2) that is activated by a new kind of love (Gal. 5:6). Miracles would flow out of His divine character, and God is love. The *dunamis* or "ability" of God is power that is inherent within His nature.

Jesus would be "great" (Lk. 1:32; see also Gen. 12:2; Mt. 1:1); He would be called the "Son of the Highest." Abraham was a priest of El-Shaddai. Moses was a priest of Yahweh, the Lawgiver. Jesus was a priest of El-Elyon, "the most high God," the God of the priesthood after the order (manner, similitude) of Melchisedec (Gen. 14:18-20; Heb. 7:1-14), the God of the "most holy place" (see Ex. 26:34; 1 Kings 8:6; Ezek. 43:10; 44:13).

Jesus was the Son of "the Highest" (Lk. 1:32). The Holy Ghost who overshadowed Mary was the power of "the Highest" (Lk. 1:35). John the Baptist would be called the prophet of "the Highest" (Lk. 1:76). The angelic host sang glory to God in "the highest" (Lk. 2:14). These verses use the Greek word *hupsistos* (Strong's #5310), which means "highest, the Supreme (God), or the heavens." The Revised Version renders it as "Most High."

This new King, Mary's first Son, the incarnate Word, would inherit the throne of His father David (Acts 2:30; Rom. 1:3-4). The greatest Son of David (2 Sam. 7) would be given all executive authority in Heaven and in earth (Mt. 28:18). His reign would be perpetual, and "...of His kingdom there shall be no end" (Lk. 1:33; see also Gen. 49:10; Is. 9:6-7). Jesus the Messiah is the only King who shall never lay aside His diadem and robes, who shall never die!

Mary's question in Luke 1:34 contains its own answer. That which is truly born from above cannot come forth "...of blood, nor of the will of the flesh, nor of the will of man, but of God" (Jn. 1:13; see also Zech. 4:6).

The Holy Ghost, the "power" or *dunamis* ("ability") of the Highest would "overshadow" Mary (Lk. 1:35). This latter word is *episkiazo* (Strong's #1982), which means "to cast a shade upon, to envelop in a haze of brilliancy; figuratively, to invest with preternatural influence." It is used to describe Jesus' transfiguration (Mt. 17:5; Mk. 9:7; Lk. 9:34) and Peter's supernatural apostolic ministry in the streets of Jerusalem (Acts 5:15). This figure of a cloud coming upon Mary is pictured by the Shekinah glory cloud of the Old Testament (Ex. 40:38; 1 Kings 8:10).

The primary difference between the previous order and this new day is that men cannot preach present truth until their hearts have been overshadowed by the Holy Ghost (Acts 16:14; 1 Cor. 2:1-5).

That "holy thing" (Lk. 1:35) born of God and Mary was foreshadowed by the Old Testament manna from Heaven, described as a "small round thing" upon the ground (Ex. 16:14; see also Jn. 6:32-35). With regard to the power of the Holy Ghost moving in the lives of the corporate Messiah, Paul wrote about the communication of our faith becoming effective by acknowledging every "good thing" that is in us by Christ Jesus (Philem. 6).

Gabriel then informed Mary that Elisabeth had conceived John (Lk. 1:36). Mary received the life of God in her womb at the beginning of the seventh month of the prophet's gestation. The time of the corporate Messiah will be marked by new life in dead wombs (Is. 54:1-2)—the end of the time of being "barren," which means "hard, firm; thus, sterile."

Don't just focus on what God has birthed in you or your ministry. This may come as a surprise, but others are expecting, too! For a fuller treatment of this truth revealed by the seven barren women of the Bible, see my book, *Sing, O Barren* (Richlands, North Carolina: Tabernacle Press, 1987).

Lk. 1:37, KJV

For with God nothing shall be impossible.

Lk. 1:37, TLB

For every promise from God shall surely come true.

Lk. 1:37, ASV

For no word from God shall be void of power.

Gabriel's declaration in Luke 1:37 is the keynote of the entire chapter (compare Gen. 18:14; Is. 55:10-11; Rom. 4:21). The literal Greek reads, "Every word of God shall not be powerless." The time of *wonder* has become the time of *witness*—Messiah cannot be silenced! Once the seed of His Word has been planted in our hearts, it must be told. He must speak. He must sing.

Lk. 1:38, KJV

And Mary said, Behold the handmaid of the Lord; be it unto me according to thy word. And the angel departed from her.

Mary consecrated her reputation, responding as the "handmaid" or "slave" of the Lord. This is the word *doule*, the feminine form of *doulos*—a voluntary love-slave unto death. May we all agree with her words, "...be it unto me according to thy word" (Lk. 1:38).

Once the woman, the Church, is filled with God and declares her covenantal commitment in fullness, the "angel," the fivefold ministry, will have done their job. We will only be needed "till..." (Eph. 4:13; see also Heb. 8:10-11).

A Time to Embrace

Eccles. 3:5, KJV

> *...a time to embrace....*

Luke's first chapter illustrates a time of *witness*. John the Baptist was conceived. Gabriel, the ruling angel, spoke to a virgin handmaiden. Mary responded to the Word of God. The portion before us (Lk. 1:39-45) recounts Mary's visit to Elisabeth and discloses key principles with regard to corporate prophetic impartation.

Lk. 1:39-40, KJV

> *And Mary arose in those days, and went into the hill country with haste, into a city of Juda;*
>
> *And entered into the house of Zacharias, and saluted Elisabeth.*

Mary arose (Is. 60:1).

She went into the hill country—the heavenlies (see Ps. 15:1; 24:3; Eph. 1:3; 2:6).

She went with "haste" or "speed; eagerness, earnestness" (compare Rom. 12:8; 1 Tim. 2:15; Heb. 6:11).

She went into a city of "Juda" ("praise")—government and order in worship (1 Cor. 14:4).

She went into the house—the local church (Heb. 10:25).

She "saluted" Elisabeth—the fellowship of the Spirit (Phil. 2:1).

The time of *witness* is a time to "embrace." The Greek word for "saluted" in Luke 1:40 is *aspazomai* and means "to enfold in the arms, to salute, to welcome." It is also translated in the King James Version as "embrace, greet" (see Mt. 10:12; Acts 20:1; Rom. 16:5-23; 1 Pet. 5:14).

This spirit of brotherly love will flow through the Church in the days of the corporate Messiah (see Rom. 12:10; Eph. 4:1-3; 1 Thess. 4:9; Heb. 13:1; 1 Pet. 2:17; 2 Pet. 1:7). This flow of love can only take place in the lives of those who have been visited by the angel, who have received the impartation of the Lord.

Lk. 1:41-45, KJV

> *And it came to pass, that, when Elisabeth heard the salutation of Mary, the babe leaped in her womb; and Elisabeth was filled with the Holy Ghost:*
>
> *And she spake out with a loud voice, and said, Blessed art thou among women, and blessed is the fruit of thy womb.*
>
> *And whence is this to me, that the mother of my Lord should come to me?*
>
> *For, lo, as soon as the voice of thy salutation sounded in mine ears, the babe leaped in my womb for joy.*
>
> *And blessed is she that believed: for there shall be a performance of those things which were told her from the Lord.*

Elisabeth prophesied and John tried to!

This kind of embrace causes that which is prophetic yet unborn to "leap" or "skip, jump" (Lk. 1:41; compare Gen. 25:22). This is especially true when a husband and wife, both full of godly seed, embrace in covenantal love. The fruit of real faith ignites the inner man, causing that which is born of the Spirit to spring up and turn somersaults. Is there a "baby"—the witness of the Spirit (Rom. 8:16)—in your spiritual womb? Is He leaping?

This kind of embrace filled Elisabeth with the Holy Ghost, loosed her tongue, and enabled her to prophesy the blessings of the Lord, thus confirming the word of the archangel (Lk. 1:28,42). Only by the revelation of the Spirit could Elisabeth know that Mary, the bride of a carpenter, was the mother of the "Lord." This is the word *kurios,* which means "supreme in authority, controller; master, owner, Sir." The Romish title, "mother of God," did not come into use until the fifth century.

This kind of embrace energized the faith of God in Elisabeth's heart as she declared that there would be a "performance" of God's promise. That which is heard in conception will be fulfilled. "Performance" in Luke 1:45 is *teleiosis,* which means "completion, (of prophecy) verification." Compare its usage with:

1. *teleioo,* which means "to complete, accomplish, or consummate" (see Lk. 13:32; Jn. 4:34; 17:4; Acts 20:24; Heb. 2:10; 5:9; 1 Jn. 4:12,17-18).

2. *teleios,* which means "complete (in growth)" (see Mt. 5:48; 1 Cor. 13:10; Eph. 4:13; Heb. 5:14; Jas. 3:2).

Like Elisabeth, we have been caught up into the spirit of this day, boldly declaring by faith and grace that God will perform His Word.

Ps. 138:8, KJV

The Lord will perfect that which concerneth me....

Ps. 138:8, NIV

The Lord will fulfill His purpose for me....

Phil. 1:6, KJV

Being confident of this very thing, that He which hath begun a good work in you will perform it until the day of Jesus Christ.

Mary's Song of the Lord

The testimony of Jesus is the spirit of prophecy (Rev. 19:10). Mary is now swept along with this anointed tide. Compare the Song of Moses (Ex. 15) and the Song of Deborah and Barak (Judg. 5), two great songs of deliverance (see also 1 Kings 4:32; 1 Chron. 25:7; Ps. 32:7; 137:3; Is. 35:10). The Song of the Lord, the "new song" (Ps. 40:3; 98:1; Rev. 14:3), is a spontaneous song from the heart as energized by the Holy Spirit (Eph. 5:19; Col. 3:16).

Lk. 1:46-56, KJV

And Mary said, My soul doth magnify the Lord,

And my spirit hath rejoiced in God my Saviour.

For He hath regarded the low estate of His handmaiden: for, behold, from henceforth all generations shall call me blessed.

For He that is mighty hath done to me great things; and holy is His name.

And His mercy is on them that fear Him from generation to generation.

He hath shewed strength with His arm; He hath scattered the proud in the imagination of their hearts.

He hath put down the mighty from their seats, and exalted them of low degree.

He hath filled the hungry with good things; and the rich He hath sent empty away.

He hath holpen His servant Israel, in remembrance of His mercy;

As He spake to our fathers, to Abraham, and to his seed for ever.

And Mary abode with her about three months, and returned to her own house.

The Messianic *wonder* has become an anointed *witness*. The anointed Seed in Mary's womb began to sing (Ps. 22:25; Heb. 2:12). She began to praise Jesus her Savior (Lk. 1:47), the One who would later baptize her with the Holy Ghost and fire (Acts 1:5,14; 2:1-4)! The wonder became a witness—Christ within will make us sing (Eph. 5:17-19).

Mary's "Magnificat," strikingly similar to the Song of Hannah (1 Sam. 2:1-10), is a powerful declaration of praise and celebration. It bears witness to:

1. The size of God's Word (Lk. 1:46). The word "magnify" means "to make (or declare) great, increase or extol."

2. The joy of God's Word (Lk. 1:47). Mary "rejoiced" or "jumped for joy" at the thought of God her Savior!

3. The depth of God's Word (Lk. 1:48). The word "regarded" means "too gaze at with pity." "Low" means "to be depressed or humiliated (in rank or feeling)."
4. The might of God's Word (Lk. 1:49). "Mighty" is *dunatos,* which means "powerful or capable," and speaks of the power of the Holy Spirit.
5. The "mercy" of God's Word (Lk. 1:50). This word means "compassion." It is the outward manifestation of pity. It assumes need on the part of him who receives it, and adequate resources to meet the need on the part of him who shows it.
6. The strength of God's Word (Lk. 1:51). "Strength" is *kratos,* which means "force, manifested power."
7. The justice of God's Word (Lk. 1:52). He has "put down" or "violently demolished" the mighty (dynasties) from their "seats" or "thrones," and "exalted" or "elevated" those of low degree.
8. The satisfaction of God's Word (Lk. 1:53). Compare this verse with Job 23:12; Jer. 15:16; Mt. 4:4; 5:6.
9. The support of God's Word (Lk. 1:54). "Holpen" means "to take hold of in turn, to succor" (Acts 20:35; 1 Tim. 6:2).
10. The faithfulness of God's Word (Lk. 1:55). God remembered His covenant (see Gen. 12:3; 17:19; 22:18; 26:4; 28:14).

I can almost hear Mary in worship as she pondered this wonder of wonders.

"I walk softly in obedience.
Listening with tender ears to Your voice,
Wanting nothing but to please You,
Unselfish in my desires.
I feel You changing me,
Speaking to my mind,
My thoughts turn often to You, Lord,
Your seed is growing inside.

"Without question, I go on,
Seeming like a fool to my peers,
At times lonely, but never alone,
I am comforted by my tears.
I was willing to follow,
You've made me to lead,
I was willing to listen,
Now I can speak!"

Author Unknown

The Seed, the incarnate Word within Mary, sang! The Wonder within her virgin womb witnessed to her and others about the goodness of her God. Praise is the language of holy people.

Mary and Elisabeth basked in this prophetic anointing for three months, until it was time for the forerunning prophet to be born.

His Name Is John

It's time for the Messiah!

Matthew 1 noted a time of *wonder*—He cannot be explained.

Luke 1 records a time of *witness*—He cannot be silenced. Gabriel, Elisabeth, Mary, John yet unborn—all sounded forth His praises.

One more voice needs to be heard. The aged priest has been speechless or mute for nine months because of unbelief. The story of Zacharias' tongue being loosed and his subsequent utterance provide the glorious conclusion to this chapter (Lk. 1:57-80). Real faith is a mouth opener (Rom. 10:10).

This story about John's circumcision is part of Chapter 14 of my book, *The Priesthood Is Changing* (Shippensburg, PA: Destiny Image, 1991, pp. 200-203). This word is reprinted here for your study.

Lk. 1:57-66, KJV

> *Now Elisabeth's full time came that she should be delivered; and she brought forth a son.*
>
> *And her neighbours and her cousins heard how the Lord had shewed great mercy upon her; and they rejoiced with her.*
>
> *And it came to pass, that on the eighth day they came to circumcise the child; and they called him Zacharias, after the name of his father.*
>
> *And his mother answered and said, Not so; but he shall be called John.*
>
> *And they said unto her, There is none of thy kindred that is called by this name.*
>
> *And they made signs to his father, how he would have him called.*

And he asked for a writing table, and wrote, saying, His name is John. And they marvelled all.

And his mouth was opened immediately, and his tongue loosed, and he spake, and praised God.

And fear came on all that dwelt round about them: and all these sayings were noised abroad throughout all the hill country of Judaea.

And all they that heard them laid them up in their hearts, saying, What manner of child shall this be! And the hand of the Lord was with him.

"The fulness of time has come; it's time for the child, the new thing, to be named or natured. This act is to be done by his father on the eighth day. All the neighbors and cousins are here; every camp is represented. Each is decked to the hilt with his own preconceived notions, his witty inventions. Each has his own prophet, primed and ready to confirm standard procedure. All have one thing in common: Each is devoted to telling the world that this new baby must be Zacharias, Jr., because the tradition of the elders, not to mention their own theology and eschatology, demands it.

"Stand back, everybody. Zacharias has moved his hand and motioned for a writing table. What excitement! We've waited 400 years for this. The last few months have been unbearable. Once again, there will be a prophet in the land.

"But wait a minute. This cannot be. Will somebody please explain what is happening here? Who's in charge? The old priest is beginning to write, and his first letter isn't Z...it's J! Maybe he's forgotten how to spell. Doesn't he know the rules of spiritual grammar?

"J...O...H...N—John. John...his name is John.

"Nobody expected this. All the neighbors and cousins are shocked, and for the first time in many years, they are speechless. But not Zacharias. The tongue of the obedient priest is loosed as he begins to declare the wonderful works of God."

Lk. 1:67-79, KJV

And his father Zacharias was filled with the Holy Ghost, and prophesied, saying,

Blessed be the Lord God of Israel; for He hath visited and redeemed His people,

And hath raised up an horn of salvation for us in the house of His servant David;

As He spake by the mouth of His holy prophets, which have been since the world began:

That we should be saved from our enemies, and from the hand of all that hate us;

To perform the mercy promised to our fathers, and to remember his holy covenant;

The oath which He sware to our father Abraham,

That He would grant unto us, that we being delivered out of the hand of our enemies might serve Him without fear,

In holiness and righteousness before Him, all the days of our life.

And thou, child, shalt be called the prophet of the Highest: for thou shalt go before the face of the Lord to prepare His ways;

To give knowledge of salvation unto His people by the remission of their sins,

Through the tender mercy of our God; whereby the dayspring from on high hath visited us,

To give light to them that sit in darkness and in the shadow of death, to guide our feet into the way of peace.

"...We have heard the Word of the Lord: The priesthood is changing! A new baby has been birthed and is about to be named. What must we do?

"It's simple. Bring the writing table. Not the tables of stone, but the fleshly tables of your heart. Bring God something He can write on. Agree quickly with the angel, the messenger (Gal. 4:14). Say 'yes' to what God has said, and He will liberate your tongue to declare the realities of the third day as He raises you up in the spirit of prophecy.

"You can't figure it out, so stop trying. This revival, the greatest outpouring of the Holy Ghost that the earth has ever witnessed, is just beginning. This new priesthood is exceeding abundantly above all you can ask or think, so it doesn't matter what you think about it. What matters most is that you have heard from Heaven and have received of His life.

"Bring the writing table. Bring your heart. Be a hearer and a doer, and agree with your Father. Don't be afraid. Step forward.

"The finger of the Holy Ghost has written a new word on your heart. This word is 'hope.' Wait just a moment. Your Father has written a postscript. It reads, 'Begin again.'

> "This time it will be different. This renaissance is new, fresh, unprecedented. His name is John...'God is gracious.' His grace is enough. The priesthood is changing, and his name is John."

Zacharias wrote, "His name *is* John" (not "shall be called John") in Luke 1:63. Gabriel had already named the prophet. Zacharias was only a recorder of the divine announcement. Covenant must be on God's terms. We can accept or reject what He has decreed, but we cannot alter it. Men are stymied in these days. Man-made plans are coming to nought. This new thing that God does is not named or natured Zacharias, Jr. We're not going back to Grandma's or Mama's day.

When the old prophet finally agreed with the words of the angel by writing them down, he was seized by the same spirit of prophecy with which Gabriel came. Some have called Zacharias' words his Thanksgiving Psalm or "The Benedictus," so named from the first word of Luke 1:68 in the Latin version. He declared the essentials of the Messianic Kingdom: mercy, holiness, truth, light, and peace.

Once a man agrees with the words of the apostolic angel, and allows the Holy Spirit to write them on the tables of his heart (2 Cor. 3:3), he will be caught up into the very spirit of that which the angel prophesied! Adam and Eve heard the voice of God walking in the "cool" or the "spirit" of the day (Gen. 3:8). John experienced the very spirit of the Day of the Lord (Rev. 1:10).

Custom demanded that Zacharias name his firstborn son after himself, after the nature of the Levitical order. But John's father had heard from God, and for the first time in a long time, the neighbors and cousins had nothing to say (Ex. 11:7 with Is. 56:10-11). Those who obey the voice of the heavenly messenger will give birth to the kind of prophetic ministry that will gain the attention of a whole nation.

Gabriel and Zacharias didn't name the new baby "Jehovah remembers"; God wasn't returning to a previous order. They named Him "gracious gift of God" because the One whom John would introduce was the Mediator of grace and truth (Jn. 1:17). Zacharias witnessed to the coming of Jesus, the Messiah, whom he declared to be:

1. The Redeemer (Lk. 1:68).
2. The Horn (power, strength) of salvation (Lk. 1:69; see also 1 Sam. 2:10; Ps. 132:17).
3. The Sum of the prophets (Lk. 1:70; see also Heb. 1:1).
4. The Savior (Lk. 1:71).
5. The Merciful One (Lk. 1:72).
6. The Covenant-Keeper (Lk. 1:73; see also Gen. 22:16-18).
7. The Deliverer (Lk. 1:74).
8. The Holy and Righteous One (Lk. 1:75).
9. The Dayspring (dawn) from on high (Lk. 1:78).
10. The guiding Light (Lk. 1:79).

Zacharias also prophesied over his own son (compare Luke 1:13-17)! The time of the corporate Messiah will see parents marking their children for God. We must tell our sons and daughters that they are:

1. Prophets and preparers (Lk. 1:76).
2. Those who give knowledge to others (Lk. 1:77).
3. Those who order their lives with mercy (Lk. 1:78).

It's time for the Dayspring from on high to "give light" or "shine upon" us (Lk. 1:79; see also Is. 9:2; 60:1-2; Mt. 4:16). Has the Word from Heaven been born in your manger?

It's time for John, who grew up alone with God, with no scribe or Pharisee to corrupt him with false doctrine, to come out of the wilderness (Lk. 1:80).

It's time for the Messiah to appear!

We have seen His season to be a time of *wonder* and *witness*. It was impossible for death to hold Jesus down because the bosom of the Father could not hold Him in (Jn. 1:18; Acts 2:24). He had to come forth—love not expressed is love not received.

We must tell the good news. God looks forward to the times we gather in corporate worship to say, "Lord, we love you." Stop fellowshipping with the back of your brother's head twice a week. Get involved in the ongoing Messianic Body, and begin to sing, pray, and prophesy! Give God something He can bless—your money, your kids, your ministry...above all, give Him your lips. Don't be afraid. It's not you who is talking; it's the Seed who is speaking. John didn't leap in the womb all by himself; he was filled with the Holy Ghost first (Lk. 1:15,41; see also Acts 2:1-4; 3:8).

But brace yourself. Once you tell it, you will be persecuted and attacked by angry, jealous religious spirits.

The time of the Messiah becomes a time of *warfare*....

Chapter Four

A Time of Warfare

"...Herod will seek the young child to destroy Him."

Matthew 2:13

The time of Messiah's first coming points to these days, the time of the unveiling of Christ in His Body, the glorious Church.

These times of *wonder* cannot be explained. The Word is proceeding from the mouth of God in this day of *witness* (Mt. 4:4). A company of prophetic messengers, pictured in Luke 1 by John, Gabriel, Elisabeth, Mary, and Zacharias, have declared the Word of the Lord. These words of spirit and life have stirred up the adversary. Such anointed witness leads to the battlefield of spiritual *warfare,* bringing persecution from religious spirits. The war—the collision of two kingdoms (Mt. 5:10-12)—begins the moment we pray, or sing, or prophesy. That's why many of us are not testifying; it's safer to keep our mouths shut. Men get into trouble for telling the truth (Jn. 17:17).

Through King Herod (Mt. 2:13-23), satan purposed to murder the Messianic Seed, the long-awaited Deliverer, the One who would bruise the serpent's head (see Gen. 3:15; Acts 26:18; Rom. 16:20; 1 Jn. 3:8). If the adversary can't destroy the Word made flesh, he wants to bastardize it. Unclean spirits, Herod's henchmen, walk the pews of our churches every Sunday to fill men's ears with distractions, lest they hear the truth and live. All spiritual warfare is over the purity of the seed.

Deut. 22:9, KJV

Thou shalt not sow thy vineyard with divers seeds: lest the fruit of thy seed which thou hast sown, and the fruit of thy vineyard, be defiled.

Again, the purpose of your adversary, the devil, is to abort or assassinate the Messianic Seed. Since the "murderer" can't kill it (Jn. 8:44; 1 Jn. 3:15), he will attempt everything in his power to defile it or deform it, to discourage it from growing and speaking. The devil is happy as long as the Heir is but a "child" (Mt. 2:13 with Gal. 4:1). An immature, disheartened, undeveloped seed is no threat to him.

Though Messiah's time is a season of *warfare*, we rejoice that the anointed Seed cannot be contaminated with mixture! The divine Seed is incorruptible, indestructible. Ungodly men have defiled the Feasts of Passover and Pentecost, but God will watch over His Word in the Feast of Tabernacles to perform it (Is. 55:11; Lk. 1:45; Phil. 1:6). This principle is specifically underscored in Luke 2 and Matthew 2 by:

1. The virginity of Mary (Lk. 2:1-7).
2. The simplicity of country shepherds (Lk. 2:8-20).

3. The prophetic witness of Simeon and Anna (Lk. 2:21-38).
4. The wisdom of Jesus at the age of 12 (Lk. 2:39-52).
5. The wrath of King Herod (Mt. 2:13-23).

What some men call spiritual warfare is but the reaping of their own foolishness (Gal. 6:7). Real Messianic conflict comes when we are persecuted for righteousness' (His) sake, when two natures, two kingdoms, collide (Mt. 5:10-12; 1 Cor. 1:30). We will be mocked, misunderstood, and hated because men love darkness rather than light (Jn. 3:19-21). Saints, stop apologizing and start rejoicing (Lk. 6:22-23; 1 Pet. 1:6-9; 4:12-16).

No Room for Them in the Inn

Lk. 2:1-5, KJV

And it came to pass in those days, that there went out a decree from Caesar Augustus, that all the world should be taxed.

(And this taxing was first made when Cyrenius was governor of Syria.)

And all went to be taxed, every one into his own city.

And Joseph also went up from Galilee, out of the city of Nazareth, into Judaea, unto the city of David, which is called Bethlehem; (because he was of the house and lineage of David:)

To be taxed with Mary his espoused wife, being great with child.

Rome, made great by violence and aggression, ruled the civilized world. A universal "decree" went forth from the godless emperor Caesar Augustus (Lk. 2:1). This word is *dogma* and means "a law (civil, ceremonial, or ecclesiastical)." It can also mean "an opinion expressed with authority; doctrine, ordinance." These man-made laws (Acts 17:7; Eph. 2:15; Col. 2:14), especially dogmatic, religious ones that go unchallenged, are the underlying cause for why all the world, then and now, is "taxed." Although this word refers to the "census" or "enrollment, register" prescribed by Rome, it witnesses to the burden of wrong government, civil or ecclesiastical. Contemporary Pharisees have "taxed" the people of God with grievous burdens (Mt. 23:4), the traditions of men (see Mt. 15:1-6; Gal. 1:14; Col. 2:8; 1 Pet. 1:18).

The whole creation is groaning under this load, waiting for the manifestation of the sons of God (Rom. 8:19-23). This is not God manifesting a people, but rather a people corporately revealing Him—*the* Son being unveiled in a vast family of sons! There is an accelerated anticipation in our hearts for the reality of the many-membered Messiah. The "hope of glory" (Col. 1:27) is God's hope, established in our hearts by His own faith, and it will surely come to pass. J.B. Phillips' translation of the New Testament renders Romans 8:19 this way: "The whole creation is on tiptoe to see the wonderful sight of the sons of God coming into their own."

It's time for Christ to be fully formed in a people. Whatever we have done to excuse ourselves from the responsibility of this high calling must cease. We must repent from casually following the Lord. The prophet

Obadiah saw the corporate Messiah as a company of "saviours" who would arise upon Mount Zion (Obad. 21)—deliverers, medicine men, curers, bringing the antidote to the antichrist.

When Caesar Augustus had his enrollment made in order to get the statistics of his empire and to raise money for its support (Lk. 2:1-5), he little knew that he was fulfilling prophecy to help build up a Kingdom that would far outlast his own throne!

It is interesting that this "taxing" began in the days of "Cyrenius" (Lk. 2:2), whose name means "wall, coldness; supremacy of the bridle." Evil systems that seek to control the lives of others are whited sepulchres full of dead men's bones (Mt. 23:27; see also Prov. 21:16; Jude 12). Cyrenius was governor of "Syria," which means "highland, elevated, a citadel (from its height)." Worldly pride energizes these works and words of men (1 Jn. 2:16). Impregnated with the divine Seed, the true Church will cast down these vile imaginations and every "high thing that exalteth itself" against the knowledge of God (2 Cor. 10:5). A religious spirit of antichrist opposes and exalts itself above all that is called God (2 Thess. 2:4).

We are living in days of fierce Messianic warfare. The first example of this truth in Luke 2 is Mary, a habitation of purity. The epitome of barrenness was her virginity (Is. 54:1-5); in her "barrenness," Mary brought forth perfection: Jesus! The "womb of the morning" (Ps. 110:3) has been reserved and sanctified to bring forth men of honor. It is like the womb of Rachel, who eventually gave birth to Joseph and Benjamin (Gen. 30:22-24; 35:16-20); or the womb of Hannah, who, after being provoked by

Peninnah, brought forth the prophet Samuel (1 Sam. 2:1-20). In the days of the corporate Messiah, Peninnah has all the money, all the facilities, and all the people (seemingly with no struggles or problems), but a man-child is about to be birthed to replace a blind, fleshly ministry that cannot discern real intercession.

Furthermore, everyone knows that tax time means pressure. In the time of the Messiah, the purpose of pressure is pushing every man into his predetermined destiny, his "own city" (Lk. 2:3), the place of his nativity. Like Mary, we are "great with child" (Lk. 2:5); the holy seed within is kicking hard, anticipating His debut.

Lk. 2:6-7, KJV

> *And so it was, that, while they were there, the days were accomplished that she should be delivered.*
>
> *And she brought forth her firstborn son, and wrapped Him in swaddling clothes, and laid Him in a manger; because there was no room for them in the inn.*

"While they were *there...*" (Lk. 2:6). It's not enough to be impacted with the anointed Seed. We must leave the comfortable place; we must move and change. Mary did not give birth on the way to the place of foreordained destiny. She could not deliver this Child in any other city. Messiah's birth had to take place in Bethlehem (Mic. 5:2). Make your calling and election sure (2 Pet. 1:10). Are you in the city of God's choosing in the time of Messiah? One thing is sure: there will be faithful shepherds "in the same country" (Lk. 2:8).

Mary had carried the divine Seed to His full term. It took Moses nine months to build the tabernacle in the wilderness (Ex. 19:1 with Num. 9:1). It took the overshadowing power of the Holy Ghost nine months to build the true Tabernacle (Jn. 1:14; Heb. 8:2) in the womb of the virgin! The number nine is the Bible number denoting *finality* (Lk. 23:44-46; Jn. 19:30).

Mary's days were "accomplished" or "fulfilled" to bring forth the Messiah (Lk. 2:6; see also Gal. 4:4; Eph. 1:10). Jesus was the Pattern Son, the "firstborn Son" (see Mt. 1:25; Rom. 8:28; Col. 1:15,18). The time has come again for the woman to be "delivered," to "travail and bring forth" (Lk. 1:57; Jn. 16:21; Rev. 12:1-5).

When Jesus came into this world, He was already in charge! Yet our King bowed low and was made in the likeness of men (Phil. 2:7-8). God humbled Himself in flesh; then Mary wrapped Him in swaddling clothes. These were long, narrow strips of cloth (probably linen) used to wrap a newborn, and were believed to ensure the correct early development of his limbs. Thus swaddling was a mark of parental care and love, while the need for swaddling revealed the humble, dependent posture of the infant (Ezek. 16:4). Linen symbolizes righteousness (Rev. 19:8). From His birth to His resurrection (Mt. 27:59; Jn. 19:40; 20:5-7), Messiah was wrapped in linen!

In the time of the corporate Messiah—Christ being formed in a people—this new and holy thing must be swaddled, properly ordered, and righteously aligned to His purposes, lest men get out of line and disqualify themselves from this new priesthood (Lev. 21:19-21; 1 Pet. 2:9). Once again, His "plumbline" (Amos 7:7-8) is being set in our midst to rectify and straighten His people (Is. 40:3-5).

The manger was a feeding trough, a stall, crib, or open box in a stable, designed to hold fodder for livestock (Lk. 2:7,12,16; 13:15). It was made of clay mixed with straw or from stones cemented with mud.

The final phrase of Luke 2:7 emphasizes that Messiah cannot be contaminated: "...there was no room for them in the inn." Because of the taxation, every place of entertainment was full. The "inn" represents the world and all that is in it (1 Jn. 2:15-17). Some men would rather make room for the devil (Eph. 4:27) than for a virgin Church filled with the spirit of prophecy (1 Thess. 5:20).

The Greek word for "room" in Luke 2:7 and "place" in Ephesians 4:27 is *topos* (compare the English word *topography*) and means "a spot limited by occupancy; condition, opportunity." It is used elsewhere in the New Testament to describe the habitations of demons (Mt. 12:43) and the place of grass, symbolizing flesh (Jn. 6:10; see also Is. 40:6; 1 Pet. 1:24). There was no room for Jesus because someone else was deemed to be more important. God would rather be born among the natural beasts than the spiritual beasts (2 Pet. 2:12; Jude 10).

The holy Seed can never be brought forth in a worldly environment. Christ and His holiness must take the stable. His entrance dignified the life of humility. The Ark cannot be brought to Zion on some new cart—the ignorant, arrogant plans of men (see 1 Sam. 6:7; 2 Sam. 6:3; 1 Chron. 13:7). In the days of the corporate Messiah, we must seek the Lord after the due order (1 Chron. 15:12-13).

The word for "inn" or "lodging-place" in Luke 2:7 is *kataluma,* and literally means "a loosening down." Travelers and their beasts would untie their packages, girdles, and sandals. The spiritual implication is that the "inn" is a place of no restraint. Those called to bring forth the Christ nature will "hold fast" and head for the manger (1 Thess. 5:21-23; 2 Tim. 1:13; Heb. 10:23).

The Simplicity That Is in Christ

The time of the Messiah is a time of *warfare*—He cannot be profaned, as depicted by the purity of the virgin.

Now we turn our attention to those who first heard the revelation of the full, threefold salvation of Jesus being Savior, Baptizer, and Lord (Lk. 2:11; see also Deut. 16:16; Prov. 22:20): simple, country shepherds—faithful men who stayed with their flocks by night. The most spiritual thing a man can do is do his job.

Lk. 2:8-12, KJV

> *And there were in the same country shepherds abiding in the field, keeping watch over their flock by night.*
>
> *And, lo, the angel of the Lord came upon them, and the glory of the Lord shone round about them: and they were sore afraid.*
>
> *And the angel said unto them, Fear not: for, behold, I bring you good tidings of great joy, which shall be to all people.*
>
> *For unto you is born this day in the city of David a Saviour, which is Christ the Lord.*
>
> *And this shall be a sign unto you; Ye shall find the babe wrapped in swaddling clothes, lying in a manger.*

When Messiah came the first time, God did not burst the good news upon downtown Jerusalem with its magnificent temple. Jehovah did not disturb the sleep of the Sanhedrin, Caiphas, or even Nicodemus. He didn't bother the neighbors and cousins (Lk. 1:58) who were still upset that John the Baptist wasn't named Zacharias, Jr. God looked for those whom the apostle Paul called "faithful men" (2 Tim. 2:2). He works the same way in these days of the corporate Messiah, in order that no flesh should boast in His presence (1 Cor. 1:26-29).

This original team of New Testament pastors were true to their calling, guarding their flock, doing their job: watching (see 1 Cor. 16:13; 1 Thess. 5:6; Heb. 13:17; 1 Pet. 4:7). The Shepherd of Israel was first adored by those who were overseeing their flocks by night on the same plains as had His forefather David in the days of his youth. It is likely that their flocks would be offered for Temple sacrifices, prefiguring the sacrificial Lamb who was born that night!

The angel of the Lord "came upon them," or "stood by them" (Lk. 2:9; see also Acts 12:7). The messenger came up on the shepherds and clothed them, and they became the message. As with Paul on the road to Damascus (Acts 26:13), these pastors were bathed with the glory of the Lord. They heard the same message as had Joseph (Mt. 1:20), Zacharias (Lk. 1:13), and Mary (Lk. 1:30): "Fear not." They were among the first to hear the gospel, the good news sent to every nation: Christ saves from fear by saving men from sin.

Messiah's first coming could only be recognized and appreciated by hungry men who discovered the Bread of life (Jn. 6:48) in a feeding trough, wrapped in the clothes of genuine humility (1 Pet. 5:5). Proud Pharisees and

Sadducees would never consider such a "sign" (Lk. 2:12; see also Mt. 12:38-39; 16:1-4; Lk. 2:34)—the "simplicity" or "singleness" that is in Christ (2 Cor. 11:3). The Pharisaical crowd would have made a religion out of the manifestation and marketed it. Their price of doves would have risen.

God will not allow anyone to contaminate the Messianic Seed. Men who build their own kingdoms only fellowship with those who join their "ship." By the strength of the law, not grace, they enslave others to religious bylaws and doctrines. The warfare is over the purity of the seed. Once a man becomes part of a real New Testament, prophetic local church, he is assailed by things that want to seduce and beguile him away from the simplicity that is in Christ. That enticement can come through his relatives, previous teachings, or even his own stubbornness.

Lk. 2:13-14, KJV

> *And suddenly there was with the angel a multitude of the heavenly host praising God, and saying,*
>
> *Glory to God in the highest, and on earth peace, good will toward men.*

These days of the corporate Messiah are bringing shakings and disturbances in the heavenlies (Heb. 12:25-29). At His first advent, the heavens erupted with sudden, militant praise—such celebration comes "with the angel" (Lk. 2:13). The voices of angels and the spirits of just men made perfect (Heb. 12:22-23) roared at the sight of the infant Lion of Judah! Those in the amphitheater stood and cheered (Heb. 11:39–12:2). This celestial "host" or "army" (called a "heavenly knighthood" by Wycliffe) camped about Bethlehem that night "praising God" (Lk. 24:53; Acts 2:47; Rom. 15:11) in the "highest" (Lk. 1:32, 35,76), prophesying peace on earth to men upon whom His favor had come to rest.

Lk. 2:15-20, KJV

And it came to pass, as the angels were gone away from them into heaven, the shepherds said one to another, Let us now go even unto Bethlehem, and see this thing which is come to pass, which the Lord hath made known unto us.

And they came with haste, and found Mary, and Joseph, and the babe lying in a manger.

And when they had seen it, they made known abroad the saying which was told them concerning this child.

And all they that heard it wondered at those things which were told them by the shepherds.

But Mary kept all these things, and pondered them in her heart.

And the shepherds returned, glorifying and praising God for all the things that they had heard and seen, as it was told unto them.

The shepherds were chosen because they mixed the Word with faith (Heb. 4:2). They did not pollute the good news with apathy or unbelief, desiring to see with their eyes what they had heard with their ears (Job 42:5). The Greek word for "now" in Luke 2:15 is *de*, a particle of urgency. These watchmen were not spiritual "couch potatoes"—those who think that if they have seen it, they have done it. These dedicated witnesses of His first advent heard it, saw it, and told it! Those who see *Him* have to tell it!

This pastoral team was diligent, striking out toward "Bethlehem," which means "the house of bread." The complete revelation of the Messiah is that we being many are one bread, one body (1 Cor. 10:17). As had Mary (Lk. 1:39), the shepherds earnestly moved with "haste" or "speed" (Lk. 2:16). After a diligent search, they "found" Him. These pastors became evangelists, sounding the good news everywhere, causing all who heard them to "wonder" or "marvel" at the announcement of Messiah's arrival (Lk. 2:18; see also Lk. 1:21,63; 2:33; 2 Tim. 4:5).

Real mothers never forget the incidents connected with the birth of their children. Mary treasured and preserved these moments close in her heart (Lk. 2:19; compare Lk. 2:51). She "kept on keeping" these things. She "pondered" or "weighed" these things in her heart; this word means "to throw together, to confer; to put one thing with another in considering circumstances." Did Mary keep a "baby book," and did Doctor Luke see it?

A Prophet and a Prophetess

Messiah cannot be contaminated! God protected the Word made flesh by the purity of Mary's womb (Lk. 2:1-7) and the faithful obedience of simple shepherds (Lk. 2:8-20).

Next is told the story of Simeon and Anna (Lk. 2:21-38), who, like Zacharias and Elisabeth, had lingered on the shores of time to bring tribute to the Messiah. The Father sealed and confirmed His Son with a pure, prophetic flow. Before God allowed this new and holy thing to be soiled by the grimy hands of a lesser priesthood, an old order that was passing away, He intercepted the divine Seed with a prophet *and* a prophetess! Pharisees wouldn't allow women into the ministry. If men are anti-women, they are anti-gospel. There can be no gender prejudice in the days of Christ, the corporate Messiah (Acts 2:16-18; Gal. 3:28)!

Lk. 2:21-24, KJV

> *And when eight days were accomplished for the circumcising of the child, His name was called JESUS, which was so named of the angel before He was conceived in the womb.*
>
> *And when the days of her purification according to the law of Moses were accomplished, they brought Him to Jerusalem, to present Him to the Lord;*
>
> *(As it is written in the law of the Lord, Every male that openeth the womb shall be called holy to the Lord;)*
>
> *And to offer a sacrifice according to that which is said in the law of the Lord, A pair of turtledoves, or two young pigeons.*

Jesus, the Pattern Son, had to experience circumcision, the badge of membership in the Jewish Church (Lk. 2:21; compare Gen. 17:12). The corporate Messiah, the Joshua generation, must be circumcised before we enter the land (Josh. 5:1-8). The reproach of Egypt must be rolled away (Rom. 8:1), the manna cease (Heb. 6:1-2), and a divine strategy received (2 Cor. 10:3-6). The end-time Church will not be defiled with worldly ways, outdated traditions, or human genius.

The "name" or nature of the Son of promise is "Jesus"—"Jehovah is salvation" (Mt. 1:21).

Mary experienced the days of "purification" or "cleansing," according to the law of Moses (Lk. 2:22; see also Lev. 12; Gal. 4:4). Jesus was brought to Jerusalem to be presented (Col. 1:28). Every firstborn son was thus redeemed by sacrifice; he would be called "holy" unto the Lord (Ex. 13:1-2,12-15). The sacrifice (Rom. 12:1) of "a pair of turtledoves" or "two young pigeons" (Lk. 2:24) (the offering of the poor, costing about 16 cents), reveals the corporate Messiah—Head and Body—Jesus and a Spirit-filled Church in His image. Mary gave the best she had to God—Him of whom the lamb she would have offered had she been rich enough, was but the type. The spiritually-blinded priest who held the infant Jesus was presenting the One who would make the Jewish altar and priesthood obsolete and no longer necessary.

Lk. 2:25-26, KJV

And, behold, there was a man in Jerusalem, whose name was Simeon; and the same man was just and devout, waiting for the consolation of Israel: and the Holy Ghost was upon him.

And it was revealed unto him by the Holy Ghost, that he should not see death, before he had seen the Lord's Christ.

There is a man, a mature prophetic ministry, within the Church. His name is "Simeon," which means "he who hears and obeys." He is righteous and genuinely pious—"just" toward men and "devout" toward God (a firstfruit of Peter's audience in Acts 2:5), awaiting with confidence and patience for "the consolation of Israel," a term denoting the Messiah (Lk. 2:25; see also Is. 40:1). Simeon lived and walked in the Spirit. He would not see death until He had seen the Lord's Christ! Until men perceive the reality of the corporate Messiah—"the Lord's Christ" (Lk. 2:26; see also Rev. 11:15)—they will never die the right kind of death (Rom. 6:6; Gal. 2:20; 1 Jn. 3:16). Many are suffering, but not for righteousness' sake. Immature sons will continue to whine until they understand the revelation of the Body of Christ.

Lk. 2:27-31, KJV

> *And he came by the Spirit into the temple: and when the parents brought in the child Jesus, to do for Him after the custom of the law,*
>
> *Then took he Him up in his arms, and blessed God, and said,*
>
> *Lord, now lettest Thou Thy servant depart in peace, according to Thy word:*
>
> *For mine eyes have seen Thy salvation,*
>
> *Which Thou hast prepared before the face of all people.*

Luke 2:29-32 has been called the *Nunc Dimittis*, which is the Latin for "Now Lettest," the first words of Simeon's prayer. Only those who have had a vision of Jesus can die in peace.

Simeon came "by" or "in" the Spirit into the temple. He saw Jesus, and "took" or "received" Him up into his aged arms. He stood in one age, and embraced another. The literal rendering of Luke 2:29 is "Thou dost release Thy servant...." The old prophet affirmed his time to "depart," to be dismissed in peace according to the promise. He had seen Jesus—God's "Salvation"—the One "made ready" for all men (Lk. 2:31).

Lk. 2:32-35, KJV

> *A light to lighten the Gentiles, and the glory of Thy people Israel.*
>
> *And Joseph and His mother marvelled at those things which were spoken of Him.*
>
> *And Simeon blessed them, and said unto Mary His mother, Behold, this child is set for the fall and rising again of many in Israel; and for a sign which shall be spoken against;*
>
> *(Yea, a sword shall pierce through thy own soul also,) that the thoughts of many hearts may be revealed.*

Simeon prophesied three distinct things over the baby Jesus: Messiah would be a light, a sign, and a sword.

First, Messiah would be the "light" of the world (Lk. 2:32; see also Mt. 5:14; Jn. 8:12). This Light would bring revelation and glory to both Jew and Greek (Eph. 2:10-18), to all "peoples" (the literal rendering of Luke 2:31).

Second, Messiah would be a "sign" continually "spoken against," or "disputed, refused, contradicted" (Lk. 2:34). Yet this One destined to suffer such persecution would be "set" or "lie outstretched" (a prediction of His crucifixion) for the "crash, downfall" and the "resurrection" of many. Messiah would be a stumbling block to many (Is. 8:14; Mt. 21:42-44; 1 Cor. 1:23), yet would raise up many to life and glory (Rom. 6:4,9; Eph. 2:6). The metaphor is a stone over which some are seen stumbling and falling, while others are rising (Is. 8:14; 1 Pet. 2:8). Judas despaired, Peter repented; one robber blasphemed Him on the cross, the other confessed; the Jewish nation fell, the primitive Church arose. Jesus is the magnet of the ages—He draws some, He repels others.

Third, Messiah, the living Word (Heb. 4:12), would be a "sword" that can pierce the soul (Lk. 2:35; see also Eph. 6:17), a flaming sword that turns every way (Gen. 3:24). Mary would taste the anguish of a nation that would reject and crucify her Son (Jn. 19:25). This sword in Luke 2:35 describes a large, Thracian broadsword, used in the Septuagint to refer to the sword of Goliath (1 Sam. 17:51).

Lk. 2:36-38, KJV

And there was one Anna, a prophetess, the daughter of Phanuel, of the tribe of Aser: she was of a great age, and had lived with an husband seven years from her virginity;

And she was a widow of about fourscore and four years, which departed not from the temple, but served God with fastings and prayers night and day.

And she coming in that instant gave thanks likewise unto the Lord, and spake of Him to all them that looked for redemption in Jerusalem.

The Jewish law required the testimonies of at least two witnesses to establish truth (see Deut. 17:6; 19:15; Mt. 18:16; 2 Cor. 13:1). "Anna," like "Hannah" (1 Sam. 1–2), means "grace." In acrostic form, G-R-A-C-E can mean **G**od's **r**iches **a**t **C**hrist's **e**xpense, or **G**od's **r**ighteousness **a**nd **c**orresponding **e**nablement. Grace, God's ability, is a progression (2 Pet. 3:18), revealed in three dimensions:

1. Grace and truth (Jn. 1:17).
2. Great grace (Acts 4:33).
3. Grace, grace (Zech. 4:7).

The message and method of the corporate Messiah is certified by divine grace.

Anna was the daughter of "Phanuel," which means "the face of God" (Lk. 2:36). She came from the tribe of "Aser," which means "happy." This aged prophetess had never "departed" or "deserted" the presence of God for over 80 years, "serving" or "ministering" to God in constant fasting and prayer, literally, "all night and all day" (Lk. 2:37). Probably married at the age of 13, Anna would by this time be about 104 years old. She came in that "instant" or "hour" to confirm Simeon's word to all those who looked for the promised Redeemer (Is. 54:5; Gal. 3:13-14). The verb for "spake" in Luke 2:38 indicates habitual action, and shows that from this time on Anna was accustomed to speak of Jesus to all those who were patiently, expectantly awaiting the real Messiah, the One who would bring "redemption" (Lk. 1:68; Heb. 9:12).

Simeon's devotion to the promised Word and Anna's steadfastness in prayer reveal the kind of prophetic witness that will operate in Messiah's season. The blending of the Word and the Spirit, like the fine flour and oil of the Old Testament meal offering, will keep this present move of God pure.

The Wisdom That Is From Above

Jas. 3:13-17, KJV

> *Who is a wise man and endued with knowledge among you? let him shew out of a good conversation his works with meekness of wisdom.*
>
> *But if ye have bitter envying and strife in your hearts, glory not, and lie not against the truth.*
>
> *This wisdom descendeth not from above, but is earthly, sensual, devilish.*
>
> *For where envying and strife is, there is confusion and every evil work.*
>
> *But the wisdom that is from above is first pure, then peaceable, gentle, and easy to be intreated, full of mercy and good fruits, without partiality, and without hypocrisy.*

The time of the Messiah is a time of *warfare*—He cannot be contaminated.

Jesus, the Wisdom from above (Jas. 3:17; see also 1 Cor. 1:30), is first pure. He stands in stark contrast to the wisdom of this world (1 Cor. 1:18-25). This is beautifully illustrated by His experience in the temple when He was 12. At this age Messiah was known as "a son of the law," and was under obligation to observe the ordinances personally.

Lk. 2:39-40, KJV

And when they had performed all things according to the law of the Lord, they returned into Galilee, to their own city Nazareth.

And the child grew, and waxed strong in spirit, filled with wisdom: and the grace of God was upon Him.

After completing the requirements of the law, Joseph, Mary, and Jesus returned to "Nazareth" (Lk. 1:26; 2:4), which means "branch, offshoot, sprout." There, as did the boy prophet Samuel (1 Sam. 2:21,26; 3:19) and His cousin John (Lk. 1:80), the fleshly Word "grew," or "enlarged, increased." Jesus "waxed strong" in spirit; He was "empowered" and "increased in vigor" (Lk. 2:40). Likewise, the corporate Messiah is to be strengthened with might by His Spirit in the inner man (Eph. 3:16). The Anointed One was filled with divine wisdom (Is. 11:1-5; Col. 2:2-3), and the "grace" or "favor" of God was upon Him (Ps. 45:22; Jn. 1:14).

Lk. 2:41-47, KJV

Now His parents went to Jerusalem every year at the feast of the passover.

And when He was twelve years old, they went up to Jerusalem after the custom of the feast.

And when they had fulfilled the days, as they returned, the child Jesus tarried behind in Jerusalem; and Joseph and His mother knew not of it.

But they, supposing Him to have been in the company, went a day's journey; and they sought Him among their kinsfolk and acquaintance.

> *And when they found Him not, they turned back again to Jerusalem, seeking Him.*
>
> *And it came to pass, that after three days they found Him in the temple, sitting in the midst of the doctors, both hearing them, and asking them questions.*
>
> *And all that heard Him were astonished at His understanding and answers.*

Jews were required to go up to Jerusalem three times a year to celebrate the feasts (Ex. 34:23; Deut. 16:16). When the Lamb of God was 12, He lingered behind at the Jewish Feast of Passover (Lk. 2:43). At this great festival, He Himself was the predicted subject (Ex. 12; Jn. 1:29). The pure wisdom of the Messiah swallowed up the religious judgment of His elders (Ps. 105:22), baffling their collective learning.

Joseph and Mary assumed that Jesus had returned with them. Having discovered that He was missing, they searched for Him among their blood relatives and well-known friends. They eventually "found" or "discovered" (after searching) the growing Seed sitting in the temple among the "doctors" or "teachers," listening and asking questions (Lk. 2:46; see also Acts 23:3). That the Boy-king was seated speaks of authority. All who heard Jesus were "astounded" or "amazed" at His "understanding," His quickness of apprehension, and His "answers" or "responses, conclusions" (Lk. 2:47).

Men still suppose they will find Messiah among their "kinsfolk and acquaintance" (Lk. 2:44), the denominational spirit of preconceived mind-sets and limited relationships (compare Lk. 1:58-60; see also Mt. 12:46-50). He can only be found in the "temple," the real Body of Christ, the one true family of God (see 1 Cor. 3:16-17; 2 Cor. 6:16; Eph. 2:21; Rev. 3:12). Jesus had virtually said, "My Father is God, and I must be in His house!"

The spiritual, Bible-based wisdom of the corporate Messiah is about to overwhelm all the learned men in the arenas of their own public forums. Present truth will find its way into every avenue of media and communication (2 Pet. 1:12). The Body of Christ is being anointed with the wisdom of Stephen, which cannot be resisted (Acts 6:10; compare 1 Kings 10:1-9). The rod of Moses will swallow up the rods of Egypt's magicians (Ex. 7:9-12; Mt. 10:16) as real apostles and prophets, secure in their own sonship, stifle the wisdom of men.

Lk. 2:48-52, KJV

And when they saw Him, they were amazed: and His mother said unto Him, Son, why hast Thou thus dealt with us? behold, Thy father and I have sought Thee sorrowing.

And He said unto them, How is it that ye sought Me? wist ye not that I must be about My Father's business?

And they understood not the saying which He spake unto them.

And He went down with them, and came to Nazareth, and was subject unto them: but His mother kept all these sayings in her heart.

And Jesus increased in wisdom and stature, and in favour with God and man.

Mary and Joseph were "amazed" or "driven out of their senses" at this time when the Messiah began to have an awareness of His *sonship* (Lk. 2:48). This word means "grief, sorrow, dejection" and comes from a root that means "to sink, go down (depression)." The phrase "about My Father's business" in Luke 2:49 is literally, "in My Father," or "in My Father's house." The Greek text can read, "In the affairs of My Father, it behooves to be Me." Jesus came to reveal the Father, the One who sent Him (Jn. 8:38; 14:7-13).

Twelve is the Bible number for divine government—the Seed had become governmental. The accountability of His being the Son of the Father was working in the youthful Messiah. The word "wist" in Luke 2:49 means "knew"; the word "must" means "it is necessary," and was often used by Messiah concerning His own appointed work (Mt. 16:21; Lk. 4:43; Jn. 3:14). Mary said, "thy father," referring to Joseph; Jesus answered "My Father," speaking of God. Luke 2:48 is the last mention of Joseph as being alive; it has been assumed that he died soon after.

Interestingly, the word for "understood" in Luke 2:50 is the root word for "understanding" in Luke 2:47. Those who do not fathom the principles of real sonship—the maturing of the heir (Gal. 4:1-7)—will find it difficult to relate to those who choose to continue to grow in grace (2 Pet. 3:18).

Jn. 1:12, KJV

> *But as many as received Him, to them gave He power to become the sons of God....*

Rom. 8:14, KJV

For as many as are led by the Spirit of God, they are the sons of God.

1 Jn. 3:1-2, KJV

Behold, what manner of love the Father hath bestowed upon us, that we should be called the sons of God: therefore the world knoweth us not, because it knew Him not.

Beloved, now are we the sons of God, and it doth not yet appear what we shall be: but we know that, when He shall appear, we shall be like Him; for we shall see Him as He is.

Yet this initial awareness of His sonship was mingled with the restraint of divine order. The boy Messiah descended to Nazareth with His parents and was "subject" unto them, though they did not understand Him (Lk. 2:51). This is the Greek word *hupotasso*. A military term, it means "to subordinate, to obey." Jesus, who knew more than the rabbis, continually ranked Himself under His parents, sanctifying His childhood, toiling at the carpenter's bench for the next 18 years! The Messiah was given authority because He stayed under authority (Mt. 28:18; Eph. 1:22; 5:24). The corporate Messiah has begun to experience genuine authority and submission in the home and the local church. As did Jesus, we will "increase" or "drive forward, advance" (like pioneers cutting through a forest) in purity in these four areas (Lk. 2:52):

1. Intellectually: "...in wisdom...."
2. Physically: "...and stature [or 'age']...."
3. Spiritually: "...and in favour [or 'grace'] with God...."
4. Socially: "...and man."

Eph. 4:14-15, AMP

So then, we may no longer be children, tossed [like ships] to and fro between chance gusts of teaching and wavering with every changing wind of doctrine, [the prey of] the cunning and cleverness of unscrupulous men, [gamblers engaged] in every shifting form of trickery in inventing errors to mislead.

Rather, let our lives lovingly express truth [in all things, speaking truly, dealing truly, living truly]. Enfolded in love, let us grow up in every way and in all things into Him Who is the Head, [even] Christ (the Messiah, the Anointed One).

Herod Is Troubled and Very Angry

A virgin womb, faithful shepherds, a sure prophetic witness, and wisdom from above had kept the Seed pure. That Messiah's time is a time of *warfare* has been revealed throughout our study of Luke 2, and is especially emphasized in Matthew 2:13-23. King Herod tried to kill the baby Messiah, the anointed Seed, the rightful King of the Jews.

Why this senseless slaughter? There cannot be two kings (Josh. 24:15; 1 Kings 18:21; Mt. 6:24). One of them must abdicate his throne. There are two kingdoms, two natures, two races, two kings—Jesus and you. Both cannot reign at the same time. Both John the Baptist and Jesus came preaching the gospel of the Kingdom (Mt. 3:1-2; 4:17). Wicked men try to kill the message of theocracy by killing the theocratic messenger.

Acts 17:7, KJV

...there is another king, one Jesus.

There is no other king but Jesus! That's why the warfare is raging in our churches, our homes, our minds, and our mouths. There are two kinds of words: those that exalt the King of kings, and those that promote the king of self. Eventually, men will have to choose between life and death, blessing and cursing. Nobody ever left your ministry over doctrine; that is but the smoke screen for their real feelings: They couldn't be in charge! When a man's beastly nature cannot have his own way, he bears his fangs and shows his claws.

Ps. 75:7, NIV

But it is God who judges: He brings one down, He exalts another.

2 Cor. 10:3-5, KJV

For though we walk in the flesh, we do not war after the flesh:

(For the weapons of our warfare are not carnal, but mighty through God to the pulling down of strong holds;)

Casting down imaginations, and every high thing that exalteth itself against the knowledge of God....

The narrative of Messianic warfare set forth in Matthew 2:13-23 reveals the pattern of casting down thrones, illustrated in the Old Testament by the downfall of King Saul and the coronation of King David. Herod's diabolical act is paralleled elsewhere in Scripture with Pharaoh's extermination of the Hebrew babies in the time of Moses (Ex. 1–2); Athaliah's unthinkable effort to kill her own grandsons, including little King Joash of Judah (2 Chron. 22–23); and the dragon standing before the sun-clothed woman to devour her manchild as soon as he is born (Rev. 12:1-5).

Herod's name means "hero, heroic." In Matthew 2, this hateful monarch represents an angry devil, "king over all the children of pride" (Job 41:34), who recognizes that he has but a short time (Rev. 12:12). He is terrified when the Seed speaks.

Herod is also a picture of the carnal mind, the arrogant king of self (Rom. 8:5-8; 2 Thess. 2:3-4). Just as Samuel completely rejected the seven sons of Jesse (1 Sam. 16), so the Holy Spirit, the Dove of God, will not anoint dead flesh. He rejected the head (human wisdom) and shoulders (human strength) of Saul (1 Sam. 9:2; 10:23) and chose a man after His own heart. All the great men of the flesh will be disqualified in the days of the corporate Messiah. God is not interested in what Herod thinks or says.

Simply put, Herod represents anyone or anything that tries to stand in the way of the "holy thing" (Lk. 1:35), purposing to destroy or usurp the rightful reign of the divine Seed in order to preserve a lesser authority. King Jesus was a threat to Herod's throne.

Herod's butchering of Bethlehem's children was in every way in harmony with his savage character. Tormented with incurable disease, and yet even more incurable suspicion, he gave this evil command among the cruel and reckless acts that marked the last months of his life.

Mt. 2:1-3, KJV

Now when Jesus was born in Bethlehem of Judaea in the days of Herod the king, behold, there came wise men from the east to Jerusalem,

Saying, Where is He that is born King of the Jews? for we have seen His star in the east, and are come to worship Him.

When Herod the king had heard these things, he was troubled, and all Jerusalem with him.

The word for "troubled" in Matthew 1:3 is *tarasso* and means "to stir or agitate (roil water)." Herod and the whole religious city were disturbed and intimidated by the news that another King was alive.

In Chapter One, we learned that Jesus Christ is the Seed of the woman (Gen. 3:15) as well as the Seed of Abraham and the Seed of David. We showed the entire Bible to be the story of Him who is the Seed:

1. From Genesis to Malachi, the Seed comes (Gen. 3:15).
2. In the four Gospels, the Seed dies (Jn. 12:24).
3. In the Book of Acts, the Seed *lives* (Acts 2:24).

4. From Romans to Jude, the Seed *speaks* (Heb. 1:1).
5. In the Book of Revelation, the Seed *reigns* (Rev. 11:15).

As you re-examine the history of the Seed, weigh especially its last three points, paralleling them with the divine "pattern" of Moses' tabernacle (Ex. 25:40) and the three major feasts of Jehovah (Deut. 16:16):

The Outer Court	**The Holy Place**	**The Most Holy Place**
Passover	Pentecost	Tabernacles
Born again	Spirit-filled	Mature
The seed lives	The seed speaks	The seed reigns
A new heart	A new tongue	A new priesthood
(Ezek. 36:26)	(Mk. 16:17)	(Heb. 7:11-14,24)

Satan purposes to contaminate the witness of the prophetic word. Like Herod, the evil one does not want the anointing to live. Our adversary panics when the Christ in you begins to mature and prophesy (Rev. 19:10). Herod, then and now, will always "despise" the prophetic word, treating it with contempt and counting it as nothing (1 Thess. 5:20). With the king of pride so troubled and angry, it can be dangerous to prophesy in the time of the Messiah.

The devil is paralyzed to hear that the anointed Seed, having learned to speak, has begun to reign. This is why he vehemently hates the gospel of the Kingdom (Mt. 24:14) and those who preach it—Kingdom living deals with governmental authority and the bottom-line question, "Who's in charge?"

Only when the Seed reigns does *change* come, for within that living Word is the power and authority to conform everything around it to its own intrinsic nature!

The anointed Seed cannot speak through you if He does not live within you. You must be born again (Jn. 3:7; 1 Pet. 1:23).

The anointed Seed cannot reign if He does not speak. Each of you, all of you, must learn to prophesy (1 Cor. 14:1-5,24,26,31,39).

Mt. 2:13-15, KJV

And when they were departed, behold, the angel of the Lord appeareth to Joseph in a dream, saying, Arise, and take the young child and His mother, and flee into Egypt, and be thou there until I bring thee word: for Herod will seek the young child to destroy Him.

When he arose, he took the young child and His mother by night, and departed into Egypt:

And was there until the death of Herod: that it might be fulfilled which was spoken of the Lord by the prophet, saying, Out of Egypt have I called My son.

The flight into Egypt had three purposes:

1. To protect the Child from His enemies.
2. To show the divine care and valuation of the holy Child.
3. To make His childhood sufferings the antiype to the history of Old Testament Israel (compare Pharaoh with Herod).

Joseph was warned by the angel that Herod was plotting against the Messiah, mankind's only hope, to "destroy" Him (Mt. 2:13). This word means "to destroy utterly" and speaks of ruin and loss. Joseph obeyed, taking his family to Egypt, fulfilling the words of the prophet Hosea (Hos. 11:1; see also Ex. 4:22-23; Num. 24:8; Acts 2:10).

The corporate Messiah has been called out of Egypt's bondage (Gal. 5:13; Eph. 4:1; 1 Pet. 2:9), out of the world and everything in it (1 Jn. 2:15-17). The word for "son" in Matthew 2:15 is *huios,* meaning a full-grown, mature son (Rom. 8:14-23). The Bible describes the end-time Church summoned out of Egypt as:

1. A worshiping people (Ex. 3:12).
2. A militant people (Ex. 12:51).
3. A disciplined people (Ex. 13:10).
4. A liberated people (Ex. 20:2).
5. A holy people (Lev. 11:45).
6. An honest people (Lev. 19:36).
7. A fruitful people (Ps. 80:8).
8. A remnant people (Is. 11:11).
9. A covenantal people (Jer. 31:32).

Mt. 2:16, KJV

Then Herod, when he saw that he was mocked of the wise men, was exceeding wroth, and sent forth, and slew all the children that were in Bethlehem, and in all the coasts thereof, from two years old and under, according to the time which he had diligently enquired of the wise men.

Mt. 2:16, NIV

When Herod realized that he had been outwitted by the Magi, he was furious, and he gave orders to kill all the boys in Bethlehem and its vicinity who were two years old and under, in accordance with the time he had learned from the Magi.

Wise men "mock" or "jeer at, deride" Herod, who was and is very "wroth" or "passionately hot with anger." He "sent forth" (the word is *apostello*) wicked men to murder the promised Seed. The days of the corporate Messiah will be marked by the appearance and devilish activity of "false apostles" (2 Cor. 11:13; Rev. 2:2).

Herod "slew" all the young sons of Bethlehem. This word in Matthew 2:16 means "to take away with violence; abolish, murder." This kind of atrocity was nothing new to this demon-possessed monarch; in his rage over rivalries and jealousies, he had already killed some of his own family. The time of the corporate Messiah's unveiling is also marked by the senseless killing of babies—abortion is America's national evil.

The barbarous Idumean diabolically planned his crime according to the time he "diligently inquired" (repeatedly) of the wise men. This word means "to be exact, ascertain; to learn carefully." As with Paul and his arduous religious training (Phil. 3:4-6), rebellious men have carefully learned the craft of killing the Seed (spiritual abortion) and vexing the Holy Ghost (Is. 63:10). They unabashedly use the Scriptures to substantiate their insane ploys. The sword of the Word of God (Eph. 6:17; Heb. 4:12) is being used to kill and not to heal in the time of the corporate Messiah.

Jeremiah's Song of Restoration

Jer. 31:15-16, KJV

> *Thus saith the Lord; A voice was heard in Ramah, lamentation and bitter weeping; Rahel weeping for her children refused to be comforted for her children, because they were not.*
>
> *Thus saith the Lord; Refrain thy voice from weeping, and thine eyes from tears: for thy work shall be rewarded, saith the Lord; and they shall come again from the land of the enemy.*

Mt. 2:17-18, KJV

> *Then was fulfilled that which was spoken by Jeremy the prophet, saying,*
>
> *In Rama was there a voice heard, lamentation, and weeping, and great mourning, Rachel weeping for her children, and would not be comforted, because they are not.*

The warfare is raging in Messiah's day. But the pure Seed will be preserved. In the midst of demonic fury and malicious carnage, the promise of God stands sure. Most realize that Matthew 2:17-18 fulfills Jeremiah 31:15-16, but few have recognized the powerful setting from which the Old Testament prophet spoke.

Although Messiah's inauguration brings about great *warfare*, the divine Seed cannot be contaminated! Herod is troubled and very angry, but at the *same time* God has gloriously promised to bring back His people from captivity. Jeremiah 30 and 31 (the context of Jeremiah 31:15-16) together are called the "Song of Restoration." These two chapters detail the promise of the New Covenant and the restoration of the glorious Church!

Jer. 30:1-3, KJV

> *The word that came to Jeremiah from the Lord, saying,*
>
> *Thus speaketh the Lord God of Israel, saying, Write thee all the words that I have spoken unto thee in a book.*
>
> *For, lo, the days come, saith the Lord, that I will bring again the captivity of My people Israel and Judah, saith the Lord: and I will cause them to return to the land that I gave to their fathers, and they shall possess it.*

The prophet was commanded to write these things in a "book" for the returning captives (Jer. 30:2; see also Ps. 40:7; Heb. 10:7). From the days of Martin Luther until now, God has been leading His people out of the captivity of religious Babylon, restoring the years (Joel 2:25), causing us to return to the "land" (Jer. 30:3; compare Eph. 1:3; 2:6).

Of historical note is the fact that Jeremiah 30–31 and every other Scripture (including Moses' words in Deuteronomy 29–30) promising that God's people would "return" to their "land" was given through the prophets *before* the Babylonian captivity of 606-536 B.C.!

C.I. Scofield mishandled these verses in his famous study Bible of 1909 to support his eschatological system of classical dispensationalism (with its undue emphasis upon natural Israel). We would do well to reconsider:

1. The pre-exilic words of Isaiah (see Is. 6:13; 10:21-22; 11:12; 27:12; 35:10; 43:5; 44:22; 49:5; 51:11; 52:8; 54:7; 55:7; 56:8).
2. The pre-exilic words of Jeremiah (see Jer. 3:12,22; 4:1; 8:4-5; 12:15; 15:19; 23:3; 24:6-7; 28:3-6; 29:10,14; 30:3,10; 31:8,10,23; 32:37,44; 33:7,11,26; 42:12; 46:27; 49:6).
3. The pre-exilic words of Ezekiel (see Ezek. 11:17; 20:34,41; 28:25; 34:13,16; 36:24; 37:21; 39:25).
4. The pre-exilic words of other Old Testament prophets (see Hos. 1:11; 3:5; 6:1,11; Joel 3:1; Amos 9:14; Mic. 2:12; 4:6; 5:3; Zeph. 2:7; 3:19-20).
5. The pre-exilic words of the prophetic Psalmist (see Ps. 14:7; 53:6; 85:1; 107:3; 126:1,4).

Each and all of these verses were *historically* fulfilled in the Old Testament post-exilic days of Zerubbabel, Ezra, and Nehemiah! Their *spiritual* fulfillment is shown in the restoration of the New Testament Church, the true Israel of God, the corporate Messiah!

At the very time Herod was massacring innocent children, God was faithfully promising to restore and preserve the Messianic Seed!

(An in-depth study of Jeremiah 30–31, including "the time of Jacob's trouble" [Jer. 30:7], which is a picture of the Feast Day of Atonement, is not appropriate to this volume. The reader is advised to see my book entitled

Principles of Present Truth From Jeremiah [Richlands, NC: Tabernacle Press, 1986].)

Jeremiah 30 is filled with the promises of:

1. Consolation (Jer. 30:1-3).
2. Tribulation (Jer. 30:4-7).
3. Salvation (Jer. 30:8-11).
4. Medication (Jer. 30:12-17).
5. Restoration (Jer. 30:18-24).

Jer. 30:17-19, KJV

For I will restore health unto thee, and I will heal thee of thy wounds, saith the Lord; because they called thee an Outcast, saying, This is Zion, whom no man seeketh after.

Thus saith the Lord; Behold, I will bring again the captivity of Jacob's tents, and have mercy on his dwellingplaces; and the city shall be builded upon her own heap, and the palace shall remain after the manner thereof.

And out of them shall proceed thanksgiving and the voice of them that make merry: and I will multiply them, and they shall not be few; I will also glorify them, and they shall not be small.

Jeremiah continues his "Song of Restoration" in chapter 31 by first describing the restoration of the city. He then declared to the surrounding nations that Jehovah had ransomed and redeemed His people. He appealed to the people to turn from their backsliding and participate in God's restoration. He celebrated the new contentment that would come upon those restored, describing the *New Covenant* out of which this new peace and security would grow. The chapter closes with a divine oath of restoration. Consider these great themes:

1. God's everlasting love (Jer. 31:1-14).
2. God's new thing (Jer. 31:15-30).
3. God's New Covenant (Jer. 31:31-34).
4. God's everlasting seal (Jer. 31:35-40).

Jer. 31:3-4, KJV

The Lord hath appeared of old unto me, saying, Yea, I have loved thee with an everlasting love: therefore with lovingkindness have I drawn thee.

Again I will build thee, and thou shalt be built, O virgin of Israel: thou shalt again be adorned with thy tabrets, and shalt go forth in the dances of them that make merry.

Jer. 31:8, KJV

...a great company shall return thither.

Jer. 31:11-13, KJV

For the Lord hath redeemed Jacob, and ransomed him from the hand of him that was stronger than he.

Therefore they shall come and sing in the height of Zion, and shall flow together to the goodness of the Lord, for wheat, and for wine, and for oil, and for the young of the flock and of the herd: and their soul shall be as a watered garden; and they shall not sorrow any more at all.

Then shall the virgin rejoice in the dance, both young men and old together: for I will turn their mourning into joy, and will comfort them, and make them rejoice from their sorrow.

Jer. 31:33-34, KJV

But this shall be the covenant that I will make with the house of Israel; After those days, saith the Lord, I will put My law in their inward parts, and write it in their hearts; and will be their God, and they shall be My people.

And they shall teach no more every man his neighbour, and every man his brother, saying, Know the Lord: for they shall all know Me, from the least of them unto the greatest of them, saith the Lord: for I will forgive their iniquity, and I will remember their sin no more.

Rachel, Dry Your Tears!

Messiah's day is a time of *warfare,* a time of weeping. Yet in the midst of Matthew 2, we have seen through Jeremiah's writings that the promise of preservation and restoration is sure.

Jer. 31:15-16, NIV

This is what the Lord says: "A voice is heard in Ramah, mourning and great weeping, Rachel weeping for her children and refusing to be comforted, because her children are no more."

This is what the Lord says: "Restrain your voice from weeping and your eyes from tears, for your work will be rewarded," declares the Lord. "They will return from the land of the enemy."

Mt. 2:17-18, NIV

Then what was said through the prophet Jeremiah was fulfilled:

"A voice is heard in Ramah, weeping and great mourning, Rachel weeping for her children and refusing to be comforted, because they are no more."

This Messianic warfare is a time of "lamentation" or "wailing" (Jer. 31:15, KJV), a time of sobbing and great moaning. The prophet portrays the trial of our faith as Rachel who refused to be comforted because her sons are gone.

Matthew 2:17-18 recounts Jeremiah's picture of the sufferings and slaughter of the Jews on their way to Babylon's captivity. The image that best embodied the prophet's feelings of sorrow for his people was that of Rachel, the great "mother in Israel," seeing from the high place of her sepulchre the shame and death of her children as she wept in her bereavement. Few images could be more striking than for Matthew to introduce a mother long dead, whose sepulchre was in nearby Bethlehem, weeping bitterly over this terrible calamity that befell her descendants.

Historically, Ramah was the place to which the prisoners were dragged, where Nebuzaradan (the captain of King Nebuchadnezzar's bodyguard) might assign some to death, others to exile, and the rest to remain bondsmen in the land (Jer. 40:1). The massacre of the Hebrew babies by Herod is thus paralleled with the time of Rachel weeping for her sons.

There is another application of Matthew 2:17-18 (with regard to the Genesis account). Specifically, who were Rachel's sons? They were Joseph and Benjamin (Gen. 30:22-24; 35:16-18)!

Dry your tears, Rachel!

In spite of Herod's rage, God has covenanted to resurrect and restore Joseph and Benjamin—who embody the spirit of sonship—in the time of the corporate Messiah!

Both Joseph ("he shall add") and Benjamin ("son of the right hand") typify Jesus Christ, the Pattern Son.

Both Joseph, the preserver of life, and Benjamin, the full brother, can also prefigure an end-time company of overcoming sons—the many-membered Anointed One, the Body of Christ!

For a fuller treatment of the lives and ministries of Joseph and Benjamin, see my book, *Principles of Present Truth From Genesis* (Richlands, NC: Tabernacle Press, 1982).

Gen. 35:16-18, KJV

And they journeyed from Bethel; and there was but a little way to come to Ephrath: and Rachel travailed, and she had hard labour.

And it came to pass, when she was in hard labour, that the midwife said unto her, Fear not; thou shalt have this son also.

And it came to pass, as her soul was in departing, (for she died) that she called his name Benoni: but his father called him Benjamin.

Jn. 16:21, KJV

A woman when she is in travail hath sorrow, because her hour is come: but as soon as she is delivered of the child, she remembereth no more the anguish, for joy that a man is born into the world.

Gal. 4:19, KJV

My little children, of whom I travail in birth again until Christ be formed in you.

There were times when the father of Joseph had given up hope of seeing his seed alive again. Jacob had been told that his son had been killed by wild beasts (Gen. 37:31-35). Rachel died giving birth to Benjamin, and later Jacob spent many long, lonely nights wondering if Benjamin would ever return from Egypt (Gen. 42–43).

Dry your tears, mother Rachel! Herod has been fierce and the labor has been hard, but your Messianic Seed will live!

Rachel died in Bethlehem, or Ephrath (Gen. 35:19); the Messiah was born in Bethlehem (Mt. 2:5-6).

"Ephrath" means "fruitful" and "Ephraim" means "doubly fruitful"; Rachel's womb was doubly fruitful, bringing forth Joseph and Benjamin. Concerning the latter, the anointed seed will not be called "Benoni," or "son of my sorrow." He will called "Benjamin," or "son of the right hand." This day of the corporate Messiah is a fresh season of joy and laughter as Rachel ceases from her weeping!

Mt. 2:19-23, KJV

> *But when Herod was dead, behold, an angel of the Lord appeareth in a dream to Joseph in Egypt,*
>
> *Saying, Arise, and take the young child and His mother, and go into the land of Israel: for they are dead which sought the young child's life.*
>
> *And he arose, and took the young child and His mother, and came into the land of Israel.*
>
> *But when he heard that Archelaus did reign in Judaea in the room of his father Herod, he was afraid to go thither: notwithstanding, being warned of God in a dream, he turned aside into the parts of Galilee:*
>
> *And he came and dwelt in a city called Nazareth: that it might be fulfilled which was spoken by the prophets, He shall be called a Nazarene.*

When Herod died, Joseph brought his family back from Egypt and settled in the city of Nazareth, again fulfilling the Scriptures. Messiah's season will be a time of going back to the Bible, especially the prophets.

The day will come when the apostolic angel will proclaim, "Arise...for they are dead which sought the young child's life" (Mt. 2:20; compare Ex. 4:19). The Greek word for "dead" is *thnesko* and carries the meaning of one breathing out his last breath.

So build a playground for the backyard, Joseph. You won't have to run from town to town anymore. There is nothing now to fear. Herod is dead! The Messiah is safe!

Put down roots in Galilee and just enjoy watching the anointed Seed grow into manhood!

Is. 26:13-14, NIV

O Lord, our God, other lords besides You have ruled over us, but Your name alone do we honor.

They are now dead, they live no more; those departed spirits do not rise. You punished them and brought them to ruin; You wiped out all memory of them.

Ps. 30:5, KJV

...weeping may endure for a night, but joy cometh in the morning.

There is no one particular verse alluded to by Matthew 1:23, the closing verse of that chapter. But the "prophets" (especially Isaiah), predicted that Messiah would be of a low and despised condition, as were the inhabitants of "Nazareth" (Jn. 1:46; 7:52; Acts 22:8), which means "branch" or "germ" (the Hebrew word is *netser*). Compare Psalms 22:6; 69:11,19. Jesus was the divine Germ from whose humble origins would grow the greatest of kingdoms (Mt. 13:31-32).

Is. 53:2-3, KJV

For He shall grow up before Him as a tender plant, and as a root out of a dry ground: He hath no form nor comeliness; and when we shall see Him, there is no beauty that we should desire Him.

He is despised and rejected of men; a man of sorrows, and acquainted with grief: and we hid as it were our faces from Him; He was despised, and we esteemed Him not.

The time of the corporate Messiah began in *wonder* and has increased in *witness*. The consequent *warfare* has been intense, but we rest in Christ, assured that the victory has been secured by His finished work. The promise of restoration is sure. The Seed is safe, kept pure by the power of God.

Having defeated every enemy, our triumphant King now sits in Zion (Ps. 2:6; Eph. 1:20-23)! Above all, the time of the Messiah is the time of *worship*. Come, let us magnify the Lord. He cannot be dethroned!

Chapter Five

A Time of Worship

"...we...are come to worship Him."

Matthew 2:2

Once again in the earth, it's time for the Messiah!

Chapters Two and Three proclaimed Messiah's day to be one of inexplicable *wonder* (Mt. 1:18-25) and unbridled, prophetic *witness* (Lk. 1:1-80)! This has brought about an unprecedented time of spiritual *warfare* (Lk. 2:1-52 with Mt. 2:13-23), as elaborated in Chapter Four. Our adversary, like the monster Herod, is most angrily determined to destroy the anointed Seed. We need not fear him, for the Messiah cannot be contaminated.

Though the battle for the purity of the Seed rages, the victory is assured and the end is secure as we rest in the glorious Person and finished work of our exalted King; ultimately, the time of the Messiah is a time of *worship* (Mt. 2:1-12)—He cannot be dethroned!

1 Tim. 6:12, KJV

Fight the good fight of faith....

2 Tim. 4:7, KJV

I have fought a good fight, I have finished my course, I have kept the faith.

The corporate Messiah must fight the good fight of faith, which must be understood in the light of that finished work: Jesus' death, burial, resurrection, and ascension.

Before we take a fresh look at the wise men and their worship (Mt. 2:1-12), we must settle in our hearts that the warfare is accomplished! Most of the thoughts given in the section below are taken from Chapters Two and Three of my book, *Whose Right It Is: A Handbook of Covenantal Theology* (Shippensburg, PA: Destiny Image, 1995).

The Warfare Is Accomplished

Our evangelical and Pentecostal heritage never emphasized the enthroned Christ. Jesus has been appointed Heir of all things (Heb. 1:2), the legal Owner of all things in Heaven, in earth, and under the earth. His throne has been established forever (Lk. 1:30-33); His priesthood (Heb. 5–7) and blood covenant (Heb. 8–10) are immutable, unchangeable. His name has been exalted above every other name (Phil. 2:9-11). Jesus Christ the Messiah is the Word who has been forever settled in the heavens (Ps. 119:89)—He will never be dethroned. The end has been secured and we are safe in Christ!

Heb. 13:8, KJV

Jesus Christ the same yesterday, and to day, and for ever.

Satan, pictured by Herod, is not God's adversary—he is ours (1 Pet. 5:8). Both Testaments proclaim Jesus' complete triumph over satan. As a man filled with the Holy Ghost, the Pattern Son defeated the evil one on his own turf (Acts 10:38). Our Lord's victory over the devil disintegrated his kingdom, denied him power over death, and divested him of all his authority.

Is. 40:1-2, KJV

> *Comfort ye, comfort ye My people, saith your God.*
>
> *Speak ye comfortably to Jerusalem, and cry unto her, that her warfare is accomplished, that her iniquity is pardoned....*

These opening verses of Isaiah 40 prophesy the beginnings of the New Testament and the coming of John the Baptist!

Is. 40:2, NIV

> *Speak tenderly to Jerusalem, and proclaim to her that her hard service has been completed, that her sin has been paid for....*

The New King James Version says in Isaiah 40:2 that "her warfare is ended." The Living Bible adds that "her sad days are gone." The gospel is the good news that Jesus has defeated sin and satan, reconciling creation back to God (2 Cor. 5:19; Eph. 2:14-18; Col. 1:19-23).

The warfare is "accomplished." This is the primitive root *mala* (Strong's #4390), which means "to fill or be full of." It is translated in the King James Version as "accomplish, confirm, be at an end, fill, fulfill, fullness." The warfare has been fulfilled. It is finished (Jn. 19:28-30)!

The war of the ages was fought and won 2,000 years ago. We must acknowledge and appropriate the bounty of His victory. To fight the good fight of faith (1 Tim. 6:12) is to arm ourselves with settled conviction that the warfare is accomplished. To participate in spiritual warfare apart from the revelatory truth that our adversary has been conquered is asking for defeat.

The Hebrew and Greek words for "faith" speak of things that are certain, settled, and established. Be assured that Jesus has finished the work. The weapons of our warfare are mighty "through God" (2 Cor. 10:3-6)—what *He* did! This is not the Joshua syndrome of "taking the land," but the higher ground of Ephesians that *He* took it! In Christ we sit, walk, and stand, postured in the heavenlies with His victory (Eph. 2:6; 4:1; 6:14). We are not fighting to whip the devil. The good fight of faith is to believe, receive, and appropriate Calvary's spoils!

The only battles the enemy has won are those in which we did not engage him. We have the right to come against satan in the name of the Lord, standing on the solid resurrection ground of Jesus' finished work. Otherwise, we will cover ourselves with sweat and beat the air (1 Cor. 9:26).

The Old and New Testaments are filled with examples of our Lord's victory over the king of darkness. Messiah went forth to crush the serpent's head (Gen. 3:15). He subdued the leader of the land of wickedness, stripping him from head to foot (Hab. 3:13). The Bible reveals eight absolutes about our glorious King, declaring that:

1. Jesus triumphed over principalities and powers (2 Cor. 2:14; Col. 2:15).
2. Jesus bound the strong man (Jer. 31:11; Mt. 12:29; Lk. 11:22).
3. Jesus slew the dragon (see Ps. 74:13; 91:13; Is. 27:1; 51:9).
4. Jesus killed the giant (1 Sam. 17).
5. Jesus judged the prince (Jn. 12:31; 16:8-11).
6. Jesus dismantled satan's kingdom (Heb. 2:14-15; 1 Jn. 3:8).
7. Jesus abolished death (see Is. 25:8; Hos. 13:14; Rom. 6:9; 1 Cor. 15:26; 2 Tim. 1:10).
8. Jesus divided the spoils (see Is. 9:3; 53:12; Zech. 14:1; Lk. 11:22; Rom. 16:20).

Jesus didn't go to hell (Eph. 4:9-10; 1 Pet. 3:18-19) to finish the victory. He went there to announce it! The complete and total triumph of our Lord is best summed up in His own words, uttered just prior to His epochal achievement at Calvary. The ancient serpent left no trailing influence upon the Rock (Prov. 30:19)!

Jn. 14:30, AMP

I will not talk with you much more, for the prince (evil genius, ruler) of the world is coming. And he has no claim on Me. [He has nothing in common with Me; there is nothing in Me that belongs to him, and he has no power over Me.]

Let Herod rage. Our King has been seated in Zion!

Ps. 2:1-6, KJV

Why do the heathen rage, and the people imagine a vain thing?

The kings of the earth set themselves, and the rulers take counsel together, against the Lord, and against His anointed, saying,

Let us break their bands asunder, and cast away their cords from us.

He that sitteth in the heavens shall laugh: the Lord shall have them in derision.

Then shall He speak unto them in His wrath, and vex them in His sore displeasure.

Yet have I set My king upon My holy hill of Zion.

Wise Men From the East

The time of *warfare* is overwhelmed by the time of *worship*. The secret of victorious spiritual warfare is to securely rest in Jesus' finished work.

Having reaffirmed His eternal victory over all enemies, we now conclude our study of Messiah's times with the story of the Magi, the wise men (Mt. 2:1-12). There are four kinds of people mentioned throughout Matthew 2:

1. The wise men, who earnestly sought the truth.
2. The chief priests and scribes, who rested in the letter of the truth.
3. Herod, who was fearfully alarmed at the truth.

4. Joseph and Mary, who were the affectionate guardians of the truth.

We turn our immediate attention to the wise men. The prophet Daniel foretold this Messianic setting, clearly defining by the Spirit those who are "wise."

Dan. 12:3, KJV

And they that be wise shall shine as the brightness of the firmament; and they that turn many to righteousness as the stars for ever and ever.

The Hebrew word describing real "wise" men in Daniel 12:3 is *sakal* (Strong's #7919) and means "to be (causatively, make or act) circumspect and hence, intelligent." It can also mean "to be prudent, to act wisely, give attention to, ponder, prosper." They will "shine" or "gleam" like the brilliancy of the heavenly expanse. These wise men are like the "stars." This is the Hebrew word *kowkab* (Strong's #3556), which means "(in the sense of blazing) a star (as round or as shining); figuratively, a prince."

The Magi were men:

1. With revelation (Mt. 2:2).
2. Led by the Spirit of God (Mt. 2:2,9).
3. With pure intentions (Mt. 2:2).
4. Who obeyed God rather than man (Mt. 2:8-10).
5. Who rejoiced in the truth (Mt. 2:10).
6. Who opened their treasures (Mt. 2:11).
7. Who were flexible in their direction (Mt. 2:12).

Mt. 2:1-2, KJV

Now when Jesus was born in Bethlehem of Judaea in the days of Herod the king, behold, there came wise men from the east to Jerusalem,

Saying, Where is He that is born King of the Jews? for we have seen His star in the east, and are come to worship Him.

The death of Herod took place in the year of Rome A.U.C. 750, just before the Passover. Jesus' birth was in the latter part of A.U.C. 749, a little more than three years before A.D. 1. Thus, the time of His nativity was around 4 B.C.

The coming of such wise men created no small stir. They arrived in "Jerusalem," meaning "habitation of peace," in search of the Prince and King of peace (Is. 9:6-7; Heb. 7:1-2). The Greek word for "wise" men (Mt. 2:1, 7,16) is *magos,* which means "a Magian, an Oriental scientist." The persons here denoted were philosophers, priests, or astronomers, dwelling chiefly in Persia or Asia. They were the learned men of the Eastern nations, devoted to astronomy, religion, and medicine. Held in high esteem by the Persian court, wise men were admitted as counselors, and followed the camps in war to give advice. Daniel became president of such an order in Babylon (Dan. 2:48).

Compare the Hebrew *Rab-Mag,* which means "chief Magian" (Jer. 39:3,13), taken from the word *rab,* which means "abundant (in quantity, size, age, number, rank, quality)." *Rab* has been rendered as "many, great, large, prestigious, powerful," and can also mean "chief" (indicating military rank similar to a general). It is used almost 500 times throughout the Old Testament (see Ex. 1:9; 34:6; Num. 20:11; 1 Kings 4:30; Esther 1:7; Ps. 48:2; 68:11; 119:162; Is. 53:12; Ezek. 1:24; 47:9-10; Joel 2:2).

In Matthew 2, there weren't three wise men (that is commonly assumed because of the three kinds of gifts, or that they represented the three great races of the sons of Noah; legend has named them Caspar, Balthasar, and Melchior); we do not know their number or names.

A careful study of Matthew 2:7-11 (see below) will reveal that the Magi eventually went to Nazareth (not Bethlehem), came into the house (not the stable), and worshiped the young child (not the baby). The time of the arrival of the wise men was after Jesus' presentation in the temple (Lk. 2:22). The appearance of His star coincided with His birth. The journey from that region vaguely called the East would occupy at least several months.

The Magi came from the "east" (Mt. 2:1-2,9). This is the Greek word *anatole* (Strong's #395), which means "a rising of light, dawn (figuratively); by implication (the east)." It also means "a rising up" or "a shoot, branch," and is so used in the Septuagint (Jer. 23:5; Zech. 6:12). *Anatole* is translated as "dayspring" in Luke 1:78 to describe the Messiah, the Sun of righteousness (Mal. 4:2), the Light of the world (Jn. 8:12).

In the time of the corporate Messiah, wise worshipers will come from the "east" in the dawning of a *new day*! The Bible reveals these worshipers from the "east" to be:

1. From the tribe of "Judah," which means "praise" (Num. 2:3).
2. Priestly singers and trumpeters (2 Chron. 5:12).

3. Those who open the doors to the house of the Lord (2 Chron. 29:3-4).
4. Righteous rulers (Is. 41:2).
5. A people who experience God's glory (Ezek. 43:1-4).
6. A people who experience the living waters (Ezek. 47:1).
7. The bright shining of God's light (Mt. 24:27).

The Son of man is Jesus, the Word made flesh. The corporate son of man is His glorious Body, the light of the world (Mt. 5:14), who are shining forth in the time of Messiah. The Daystar is arising within the hearts of His people (2 Pet. 1:19). This indwelling Christ nature is the wisdom of God (1 Cor. 1:24; Col. 2:3). Wise men are arising to walk in this unprecedented season of His shining (Is. 60:1; Eph. 5:14) described in Matthew's Gospel.

Mt. 24:27, KJV

For as the lightning cometh out of the east, and shineth even unto the west; so shall also the coming of the Son of man be.

The word for "lightning" here is *astrape* (Strong's #796), which means "lightning; by analogy, glare." It is used in Matthew 28:3, Luke 10:18; 17:24; Revelation 4:5; 8:5; 11:19; and 16:18, and is also translated one time in the King James Version as "bright shining."

Lk. 11:36, KJV

If thy whole body therefore be full of light, having no part dark, the whole shall be full of light, as when the bright shining of a candle doth give thee light.

As we ascend into Zion through our worship, the whole Body of the corporate Messiah shall be illumined with the understanding of resurrection life and light!

1 Sam. 14:27, KJV

But Jonathan…put forth the end of the rod that was in his hand, and dipped it in an honeycomb, and put his hand to his mouth; and his eyes were enlightened.

Eph. 1:18, KJV

The eyes of your understanding being enlightened; that ye may know….

The "candle" mentioned in Luke 11:36 was a portable "lamp" usually set on a stand (see Mt. 5:15; 6:22; Lk. 12:35; Jn. 5:35; Rev. 21:23; 22:5). This candlestick or lampstand is the Church (Rev. 1:20). For an in-depth study of the seven-branched golden lampstand and "the seven Spirits of God," depicting the fullness of the Spirit (see Rev. 1:4; 3:1; 4:5; 5:6), see my book *The Tabernacle of Moses* (Richlands, NC: Tabernacle Press, 1978).

"…For we have seen His star…" (Mt. 2:2); this is the "morning star" (Rev. 2:28). The word for "star" (Mt. 2:2,7,9-10) is *aster* and means "a star (as strown over the sky)." Among the ancients, the appearance of a new star or comet was regarded as an omen of some remarkable event. Perhaps the wise men had been aware of Balaam's ancient prophecy.

Num. 24:17, KJV

I shall see Him, but not now: I shall behold Him, but not nigh: there shall come a Star out of Jacob, and a Sceptre shall rise out of Israel….

That the wise men came from the "east" is no small study. To further facilitate the reader, the information below is taken from Volume 2 of *Understanding Types, Shadows, and Names: A Biblical Guide* (Shippensburg, PA: Destiny Image, due for release in 1997).

The primary meaning of *dawn* (*dayspring*) is a new day, new hope, and new promise. Dawn is the first appearance of light in the morning as the sun rises.

"Dawn" is from the Hebrew *'alah* (Strong's #5927), which means "to ascend." This is the same word used to describe the "burnt offering" and is akin to "El-Elyon," the "Most High God." Two New Testament words for "dawn" are *epiphosko* (Strong's #2020), which means "to begin to grow light"; and *diaugazo* (Strong's #1306), which means "to glimmer through," or "to shine through."

Again, Jesus Christ is the "day star" (2 Pet. 1:19), the "Sun of righteousness" who arises with healing in His rays (Mal. 4:2), the "light of the world" (Jn. 8:12). Zacharias, the father of John the Baptist, described Him as "the dayspring from on high" who has mercifully visited this planet "to give light" to them who sit in darkness (Lk. 1:78-79). The wise men followed His star in the east (Mt. 2:1-9). Heaven's "dayspring" was under the commandment of the Father (Jn. 8:29; Heb. 5:7-9). Hosea prophesied that His "going forth is prepared as the morning" (Hos. 6:3).

Peter admonished every true worshiper, "We have also a more sure word of prophecy; whereunto ye do well that ye take heed, as unto a light that shineth in a dark place, until the day dawn, and the day star arise in your hearts" (2 Pet. 1:19). The glorious Church is arising in the earth, conformed to His image, "clear as the sun" (Song 6:10). This great army of people is like "the morning spread upon the mountains" (Joel 2:2). As sons of light (Eph. 5:8), we have begun to arise and shine in this new day (Is. 60:1; Eph. 5:14).

Alabaster, the Perfume of Worship

Mt. 2:1-2, NIV

After Jesus was born in Bethlehem in Judea, during the time of King Herod, Magi from the east came to Jerusalem

and asked, "Where is the one who has been born king of the Jews? We saw His star in the east and have come to worship Him."

The time of the Messiah is a time of *worship*. The wise men were a firstfruits of the non-Jewish world, the earnest of the future ingathering of all nations (Is. 60:3,6; Mt. 24:14).

The Hebrew word for "worship" means "to depress, prostrate (in homage); bow down." The Greek *proskuneo* (Strong's #4352) means "to kiss, like a dog licking his master's hand; to crouch to, prostrate oneself in homage (do reverence to, adore)."

When Jesus was at Bethany in the house of Simon the leper, there came a woman with an alabaster box of precious spikenard. She opened the box and poured it on His head (Mk. 14:3)—a vivid picture of true worship. Jesus Himself explained, "...she is come aforehand to anoint My body to the burying...Wheresoever this gospel shall be preached throughout the whole world, this also that she hath done shall be spoken of for a memorial of her" (Mk. 14:8-9; see also Mt. 26:6-13).

Jesus Christ was Heaven's alabaster box sealed by the Father (Jn. 6:27). On the cross, He was broken and spilled out. At His resurrection, He broke the seal (Mt. 27:66). In His eternal triumph, the Lion of the tribe of Judah prevailed to break and loose the seals (Rev. 5:5). Worthy is the Lamb who is to be worshiped (Rev. 5:9-14)!

Luke's similar account also narrates the essence of true worship (Lk. 7:36-50). Jesus' ensuing lesson to Simon revealed that those who love Him most are those to whom He forgave most—"to whom little is forgiven, the same loveth little" (Lk. 7:42-43,47). The nature of true worship in the Old Testament is sacrifice (Gen. 22:5; Rom. 12:1-2). Moses said that we are to "worship no other god: for the Lord, whose name is Jealous, is a jealous God" (Ex. 34:14). The Psalmist affirmed, "O come, let us worship and bow down: let us kneel before the Lord our maker" (Ps. 95:6). In the New Testament, there are three kinds of "worship" that are not acceptable to God:

1. Vain worship (Mt. 15:7-9).
2. Ignorant worship (Acts 7:22-28).
3. Will worship (Col. 2:18-23).

The perfect Worshiper told us that "God is a Spirit: and they that worship Him must worship Him in spirit [from his heart] and in truth [according to the Word of God]" (Jn. 4:24).

Worship the Shepherd-King

Mt. 2:3-6, KJV

When Herod the king had heard these things, he was troubled, and all Jerusalem with him.

And when he had gathered all the chief priests and scribes of the people together, he demanded of them where Christ should be born.

And they said unto him, In Bethlehem of Judaea: for thus it is written by the prophet,

And thou Bethlehem, in the land of Juda, art not the least among the princes of Juda: for out of thee shall come a Governor, that shall rule My people Israel.

Mt. 2:6, NIV

But you, Bethlehem, in the land of Judah, are by no means least among the rulers of Judah; for out of you will come a ruler who will be the shepherd of My people Israel.

When Herod heard that there was another King, he was "troubled" or "agitated" (Mt. 2:3). He gathered the "chief priests and scribes," the same ones who would later crucify Messiah (see Mt. 16:21; 21:15; Lk. 22:2; 23:10). The "chief priests" included the high priest and his deputies as well as the heads of the 24 orders divided by David (1 Chron. 23–24). The "scribes" (mostly Pharisees) were learned men skilled in interpreting the law (Mt. 22:35; Lk. 5:17). The wicked king "demanded" or "inquired" of them where Messiah would be born (Mt. 2:4).

Christ would be born in "Bethlehem" (Mt. 2:6), which means "house of bread." "Judaea" means "praise." Our heavenly Boaz, the Kinsman-Redeemer, came from Bethlehem (Ruth 2:4), the city of David (1 Sam. 20:6; Lk. 2:4; Jn. 7:42). Messiah is from Bethlehem-Judah; the Bread of life, the meal offering from above, was a mysterious mingling of earth's fine flour and Heaven's oil.

Mic. 5:2, KJV

But thou, Bethlehem Ephratah, though thou be little among the thousands of Judah, yet out of thee shall He come forth unto Me that is to be ruler in Israel; whose goings forth have been from of old, from everlasting.

Matthew 2:6 is the fulfillment of Micah 5:2. The Targum of Micah 5:2 (translations of parts of the Old Testament from Hebrew into Aramaic) inserts the words, "Out of thee the Messiah shall come." Bethlehem was small among the "princes" or "leaders, rulers" of Judah. Yet Messiah would be Israel's "governor." This word is *hegeomai* (Strong's #2233), which means "to lead, command (with official authority)." It can also mean "to lead the way, to preside, rule, be the chief." Jesus is Ruler and King.

Messiah would "rule" or "shepherd" the people of God (see Rev. 2:27; 7:17; 12:5; 19:15).

Is. 40:10-11, KJV

Behold, the Lord God will come with strong hand, and His arm shall rule for Him: behold, His reward is with Him, and His work before Him.

He shall feed His flock like a shepherd: He shall gather the lambs with His arm, and carry them in His bosom, and shall gently lead those that are with young.

Jesus, the Way (Jn. 14:6), is the chief Singer (Hab. 3:19), the chief Cornerstone (Eph. 2:20; 1 Pet. 2:6), and the chief Shepherd (1 Pet. 5:4). The corporate Messiah, His mature Church, will become the head and not the tail (Deut. 28:13; see also Is. 60:5-15; Rev. 21:23-26).

Mt. 2:7-10, KJV

Then Herod, when he had privily called the wise men, enquired of them diligently what time the star appeared.

And he sent them to Bethlehem, and said, Go and search diligently for the young child; and when ye have found Him, bring me word again, that I may come and worship Him also.

When they heard the king, they departed; and, lo, the star, which they saw in the east, went before them, till it came and stood over where the young child was.

When they saw the star, they rejoiced with exceeding great joy.

Herod's inquiry was like the kiss of Judas. He privately summoned the Magi to learn accurately the exact time at which the star "appeared" (Mt. 2:7; compare Mt. 2:16). This is the Greek word *phaino* (Strong's #5316), which means "to lighten (shine), show." It is taken from *phos* or *phao,* which means "to shine or make manifest, especially the rays; luminousness," and is translated in the King James Version as "fire, light." Compare Matthew 1:20; 2:13, 19; 24:27; John 1:5; Philippians 2:15; Colossians 3:4; and First John 2:8.

After the wise men departed from Herod, the star that led them from the east went "before" (kept on in front of) them until it stood over the Christchild (Mt. 2:9). This is the word *proago,* which means "to lead forward (magisterially) to precede" (Lk. 4:1; Rom. 8:14; Gal. 5:18). When the "saw" or "knew" the star, they rejoiced exceedingly (Mt. 2:10; compare Lk. 1:14; 2:10).

Gold, Frankincense, and Myrrh

Mt. 2:11, KJV

And when they were come into the house, they saw the young child with Mary His mother, and fell down, and worshipped Him: and when they had opened their treasures, they presented unto Him gifts; gold, and frankincense, and myrrh.

The patristic interpretation by the early Church fathers of these gifts is interesting: the gold, of kingly power; the frankincense, of divinity; the myrrh, of death and embalmment.

As noted, the wise men arrived at the house in Nazareth when Jesus was a "young child." This is *paidion,* which means "a little or young child." The Magi "saw" both Messiah and His mother; this word means "to find, to learn or discover." In the days of the corporate Messiah, wise men will discover the truths concerning both "brideship" (pictured in Mary) and sonship (pictured in the Pattern Son). These twin truths are explored in my book, *Principles of Present Truth From Ezra, Nehemiah, and Esther* (Richlands, NC: Tabernacle Press, 1985).

The wise men "fell down" and worshiped Jesus, just as the "four and twenty elders fell down before the Lamb" (Rev. 4:10; 5:8,14; see also Mt. 4:9; 18:26; Lk. 17:16; 1 Cor. 14:25). They opened up their "treasures," or "deposit, wealth." This is the Greek word *thesauros* and means "a place of safe keeping" (see Mt. 6:19-20; 12:35; 13:52; 2 Cor. 4:7). The Psalmist said it best.

Ps. 119:11, KJV

Thy word have I hid in mine heart....

In Matthew 2:11, the Magi "presented" or "brought" unto Messiah their "gifts" or "sacrifices" (see Rom. 12:1; Phil. 2:17; Heb. 13:15-16; 1 Pet. 2:5):

1. Gold, the price of worship.
2. Frankincense, the purity of worship.
3. Myrrh, the pain of worship.

Job 23:10, KJV

But He knoweth the way that I take: when He hath tried me, I shall come forth as gold.

Zech. 13:9, KJV

And I will bring the third part through the fire...and will try them as gold is tried....

Mal. 3:3, KJV

...and He shall purify the sons of Levi, and purge them as gold....

Wise men give Him gold, the *price* of worship. Gold symbolizes the divine nature (2 Pet. 1:4). The Psalmist described the Bride of Christ as a queen standing clothed in gold (Ps. 45:9,13). The golden candlestick pictures the Church, the corporate Messiah (Ex. 25:31; Zech. 4:2; Rev. 1:20). Vessels of gold are vessels of honor (2 Tim. 2:20). The New Jerusalem, the city of the living God, is made of pure gold (Heb. 12:22-23; Rev. 21:18).

Gold, the price of worship, requires the fiery "furnace" (Prov. 17:3; Dan. 3:6); it is there that we are conformed to His image. We only give Him what is already

His (Hag. 2:8). Wise men who glorify the Christchild with gold are familiar with the fire:

1. Some are by the fire (Mk. 14:54; Lk. 22:54-61).
2. Some are under the fire (Ex. 9:23-26; Ps. 78:47-48; 105:32).
3. Some are in the fire (Dan. 3:20-25).
4. Some are on fire (Ps. 104:2; Acts 9:3).
5. Some are as fire (Heb. 12:29; 1 Jn. 4:17).

To worship Him with gold is to present Him with a life that has been transformed into the image of God.

Ex. 30:34, KJV

...Take...these sweet spices...with pure frankincense....

Lev. 24:7, KJV

And thou shalt put pure frankincense upon each row, that it may be on the bread....

Rev. 19:8, KJV

And to her was granted that she should be arrayed in fine linen, clean and white: for the fine linen is the righteousness of saints.

Wise men give Him frankincense, the *purity* of worship. The root Hebrew word for "frankincense" is *laban*, which means "to be (or become) white." White is the Bible color denoting righteousness or purity. Frankincense is pure white, just like Jesus. This aromatic gum resin was collected from a tree that was pierced during the night, allowing the sap to flow out during the dark hours. Wise men worship Him in every circumstance.

Frankincense was an ingredient of the sacred anointing oil (Ex. 30:34). It was used in sacrificial offerings (Lev. 2:1), as a fumigant on the golden altar of incense during animal sacrifices (Ex. 30:7), and as a perfume (Song 3:6).

Frankincense was placed for seven days on top of the 12 loaves on the table of showbread (Lev. 24:7). When the bread was consumed by the priests every sabbath, its frankincense was then put on the golden altar, its sweet odor perfuming the entire Holy Place. The height of worship is found in the corporate priestly experience, around the table of the Lord (1 Cor. 10:17). The real purity of worship is produced by meaningful covenantal relationships.

The Magi's gift revealed the wisdom that is pure (Jas. 3:17; see also Mt. 5:8; Phil. 4:8; Tit. 1:15; 1 Jn. 3:3).

To worship Him with frankincense is to present Him with a life that has been made pure and white through suffering for righteousness' sake.

Esther 2:12, KJV

...(for so were the days of their purifications accomplished...six months with oil of myrrh...).

Ps. 45:8, KJV

All Thy garments smell of myrrh...out of the ivory palaces....

Mk. 15:23-24, KJV

And they gave Him to drink wine mingled with myrrh: but He received it not.

And when they had crucified Him....

Wise men give Him myrrh, the *pain* of worship. Myrrh points to the death of the cross, the denial of self, laying down one's life for others (1 Jn. 3:16). The "mountain of myrrh" (Song 4:6) is Mount Calvary (Lk. 23:33). The root Hebrew word of "myrrh" is *marar*, which means "to trickle, to be bitter." Myrrh was extracted from a gum tree. It was bitter to the taste but had a fragrant odor.

Myrrh was also an ingredient in the anointing oil (Ex. 30:23). It was used as perfume (Ps. 45:8), in purification rites for women (Esther 2:12), and in embalming (Jn. 19:39).

To worship Him with myrrh is to present Him with a life that has been made conformable to His death—the death of the cross.

The gifts of the wise men characterize the glorious Church, the corporate Messiah, conformed to the image of Christ.

Song 3:6, NIV

Who is this coming up from the desert like a column of smoke, perfumed with myrrh and incense made from all the spices of the merchant?

2 Cor. 2:14-16, NIV

But thanks be to God, who always leads us in triumphal procession in Christ and through us spreads everywhere the fragrance of the knowledge of Him.

For we are to God the aroma of Christ among those who are being saved and those who are perishing.

To the one we are the smell of death; to the other, the fragrance of life....

Finally, that the Magi gave Messiah gold and costly spices also reveals that the end-time Church, the corporate Messiah, will receive the wealth of the nations! To facilitate further study, we note this truth throughout the Scriptures (see Gen. 2:11-12; 13:2; Ex. 3:22; 12:35-36; 41:42; Deut. 8:18; 2 Sam. 8:11; 1 Kings 6:21-22; 10:1-10; 1 Chron. 22:14-16; 2 Chron. 1:12-17; 9:1-24; Ezra 1:1-11; Job 22:24; 42:10-11; Prov. 13:22; Song 3:9-10; Is. 23:18; 60:1-17; 61:6; Dan. 5:16; Hag. 2:6-9; Zech. 14:14-21; Rev. 21–22).

Another Way

Mt. 2:12, KJV

And being warned of God in a dream that they should not return to Herod, they departed into their own country another way.

Once the Magi had presented their gifts to the Messiah, they began to return to their own country (Lk. 8:39).

As with Joseph (Mt. 1:20), they were "warned" or "admonished" not to return to Herod. Thus they "departed" or "withdrew" *another way*. The word for "way" is *hodos* and means "a road; a progress (the route, act, or distance); figuratively, a mode or means." It can also mean "path, journey, or highway."

The wise men were delivered once and for all from Herod (see Chapter Four). Once they had been in the presence of the real King of the Jews, they experienced a *change* in their walk, their lifestyle!

The corporate Messiah is being transformed by true worship to order their lives "another way." Wise men walk a different path. This highway to Zion—real Kingdom living—is clearly marked by the reality of:

1. Another temple (Mk. 14:58).
2. Another form (Mk. 16:12).
3. Another Comforter (Jn. 14:16).
4. Another King (Acts 17:7).
5. Another glory (1 Cor. 15:41).
6. Another priest (Heb. 7:11,15).
7. Another tribe (Heb. 7:13).
8. Another angel (Rev. 7:2; 8:3; 10:1; 14:6-18; 18:1).
9. Another wonder (Rev. 12:3).
10. Another sign (Rev. 15:1).
11. Another voice (Rev. 18:4).
12. Another book (Rev. 20:12).

And of His Kingdom There Shall Be No End

The time of the Messiah is a time of *worship*—He cannot be dethroned!

As stated, our evangelical and Pentecostal roots never emphasized the enthroned Christ. We were ever fighting the devil, never quite sure of ourselves. Our adolescent double-mindedness kept us frustrated, insecure, and filled with shame and condemnation.

We were spiritual schizophrenics beset with Adam's sin-consciousness. Like the Shulamite in her immaturity, we saw ourselves black in Adam and beautiful in Christ

(Song 1:5). In that unenlightened state, we were like children picking the buds from a flower, flirting in our minds with a distant, impersonal God—"He loves me, He loves me not..." There are not two natures in the believer; as new creatures in Christ, we have but one—His! We are but struggling with the memory of sin.

Now that we have entered the holiest of all by the blood of the Lamb, we rest in His person and finished work. The end is secure. Jesus is our Anchor within the veil, the Rock who will never be moved.

Like the young prophet Elisha who saw Elijah in his ascension, and who consequently received the double portion (the portion of the firstborn), true sons have beheld the Messiah in His lifting up and exaltation...as He is...King over all!

The Lord Jesus Christ isn't *going* to be King of kings—He already is! Love is not a feeling; love is a choice—we choose to worship Him. Whatever our present circumstance or eschatological grid, we are assured that the end is secure and that Jesus is Lord! Magnify the Lord! Make Him bigger than anything you have faced, anything you think you are facing, or anything you will face!

Both Testaments proclaim that His Kingdom rule and authority shall never end!

Ex. 15:18, KJV

The Lord shall reign for ever and ever.

Ps. 145:13, KJV

Thy kingdom is an everlasting kingdom, and Thy dominion endureth throughout all generations.

Ps. 146:10, KJV

The Lord shall reign for ever, even thy God, O Zion, unto all generations. Praise ye the Lord.

Dan. 7:14, KJV

And there was given Him dominion, and glory, and a kingdom, that all people, nations, and languages, should serve Him: His dominion is an everlasting dominion, which shall not pass away, and His kingdom that which shall not be destroyed.

Dan. 7:27, KJV

And the kingdom and dominion, and the greatness of the kingdom under the whole heaven, shall be given to the people of the saints of the most High, whose kingdom is an everlasting kingdom, and all dominions shall serve and obey Him.

Mic. 4:7, KJV

And I will make her that halted a remnant, and her that was cast far off a strong nation: and the Lord shall reign over them in mount Zion from henceforth, even for ever.

2 Pet. 1:11, KJV

For so an entrance shall be ministered unto you abundantly into the everlasting kingdom of our Lord and Saviour Jesus Christ.

Rev. 11:15, KJV

And the seventh angel sounded: and there were great voices in heaven, saying, The kingdoms of this world are become the kingdoms of our Lord, and of His Christ; and He shall reign for ever and ever.

Messiah has come! There was born in the city of David a Savior, who is Christ the Lord!

Is. 9:6-7, KJV

For unto us a child is born, unto us a son is given: and the government shall be upon His shoulder: and His name shall be called Wonderful, Counsellor, The mighty God, The everlasting Father, The Prince of Peace.

Of the increase of His government and peace there shall be no end, upon the throne of David, and upon His kingdom, to order it, and to establish it with judgment and with justice from henceforth even for ever. The zeal of the Lord of hosts will perform this.

Lk. 1:30-33, KJV

And the angel said unto her, Fear not, Mary: for thou hast found favour with God.

And, behold, thou shalt conceive in thy womb, and bring forth a son, and shalt call His name JESUS.

He shall be great, and shall be called the Son of the Highest: and the Lord God shall give unto Him the throne of His father David:

And He shall reign over the house of Jacob for ever; and of His kingdom there shall be no end.

Chapter Six

Epilogue

Phil. 3:1, AMP

...To keep writing to you [over and over] of the same things is not irksome to me, and it is [a precaution] for your safety.

2 Pet. 1:12, KJV

Wherefore I will not be negligent to put you always in remembrance of these things, though ye know them, and be established in the present truth.

The time of the Messiah has come! It's time for Him to be revealed in you (Gal. 1:16)!

We have taken a fresh look at the Christmas story (the time of Messiah's first advent) in the light of present truth. Our scriptural backdrop has been Matthew 1–2 and Luke 1–2, four chapters that provide a prophetic panorama of the end-time Church, a divinely begotten people in whom Christ is being fully formed (Gal. 4:19; Phil. 1:6; Col. 1:27).

Chapter One introduced this message, declaring that the terms "Messiah" and "Christ" are synonymous, that the mystery of "Christ" in the New Testament reveals Him to be one new creation Man—Head and Body—Jesus in union with His Church, one anointed Seed.

Chapter Two showed the time of the Messiah to be a time of *wonder*—He cannot be explained. Great is the mystery of godliness: God was manifested in the flesh. Something unprecedented happened: A virgin conceived! Divine life has been birthed in our lives and churches in dimensions that boggle the mind, and all without the help of man.

In Chapter Three, the *wonder* became a *witness*—Messiah cannot be silenced. The unexpected birth of John the Baptist, the apostolic message of the archangel Gabriel, the magnificant song of Mary, the spontaneous prophetic utterances of Elisabeth and Zacharias—all were manifestations that the Seed was speaking.

In Chapter Four, the *witness* brought us into *warfare*—Messiah cannot be contaminated. The purity of the Seed will be preserved. This was illustrated by the virgin's womb; the integrity of simple country shepherds; the protective, confirming words of the prophet Simeon and the prophetess Anna; the confounding of religious spirits by the preteen Messiah; and especially the demonic fury of wicked King Herod in his intent to destroy the royal Seed.

In Chapter Five, we rejoiced to know that the victory has been won and the end secured; the time of the Messiah is a time of *worship*—He cannot be dethroned. The wise men came from the east and poured out their treasures at the feet of the Anointed One. Their gold was the price of worship, their frankincense the purity of worship, and their myrrh the pain of worship. Worship is life-changing. Men will walk and live differently after having been in the presence of the King of kings, whose Kingdom shall have no end! They will return to their daily lives and businesses another way.

Messiah's day is a time of wonder, witness, warfare, and worship.

Mal. 3:2, NIV

But who can endure the day of His coming? Who can stand when He appears?...

Two Angels in White

The American Church is a flock of spiritual couch potatoes. When our favorite team wins the game, we jump up and shout, "We won! We won!"

No, *they* won! *We* watched! They paid the price of victory. We observed from a safe distance.

We think that if we have *seen* it, we have *done* it.

Jn. 20:3-5, KJV

Peter therefore went forth, and that other disciple, and came to the sepulchre.

So they ran both together: and the other disciple did outrun Peter, and came first to the sepulchre.

And he stooping down, and looking in, saw the linen clothes lying; yet went he not in.

John, who outran Peter to the tomb, made the same mistake on resurrection morning. The disciple whom

Jesus loved was the first to see the reality of resurrection life, but did not enter in.

In the past 40 years, classical Kingdom-sonship theology outran its fellow disciples in the grasp of revelation knowledge. Some of us were the first to see present truth, the present reality of the Kingdom of God and the consummate purpose for the Church to be realized in the Feast of Tabernacles, but did not mix the Word with faith. Now the rest of our brethren are receiving a fresh understanding of the prophetic Scriptures.

Heb. 4:6, KJV

Seeing therefore it remaineth that some must enter therein, and they to whom it was first preached entered not in because of unbelief.

Heb. 4:9, KJV

There remaineth therefore a rest to the people of God.

The Body of Christ must enter in *together* as the corporate Messiah. What Mary Magdalene beheld that resurrection morning vividly clarifies the secret to our becoming one in the day when Christ is fully formed in a people (Acts 17:20-26; Eph. 4:1-7).

Jn. 20:11-12, KJV

But Mary stood without at the sepulchre weeping: and as she wept, she stooped down, and looked into the sepulchre,

And seeth two angels in white sitting, the one at the head, and the other at the feet, where the body of Jesus had lain.

Two angels, two messengers...two messages.

Both messengers were in white...both messages, like linen, are righteous (Rev. 19:8)...*both* are right!

The messenger at the "head" (Jn. 20:12) pictorially embodies a company of real prophets, speaking forth deep, revelatory truth.

The messenger at the "feet" represents a company of real evangelists, the foot soldiers of the Church.

Our local church is powerful in revelation knowledge but pitifully weak in evangelism. A lot of folks think we are wrong, and some deem us crazy. They do not know or understand us. I declare that we are dressed in "white"—what we are *saying* is righteous.

Other local assemblies are powerful in evangelism yet woefully ignorant of present truth. We think they are wrong and need to hear what God is saying by His Spirit. We do not know or understand them. I acknowledge that they are dressed in "white"—what they are *doing* is righteous.

1 Cor. 12:21, NIV

> *The eye cannot say to the hand, "I don't need you!" And the head cannot say to the feet, "I don't need you!"*

Mary Magdalene saw *both* angels, both messages—upreach and outreach. Until these two ministries—one at the head and the other at the feet—sit down together, the Body of Christ will never rise from the dead!

Lk. 2:15-17, KJV

> *And it came to pass, as the angels were gone away from them into heaven, the shepherds said one to another,*

Let us now go even unto Bethlehem, and see this thing which is come to pass, which the Lord hath made known unto us.

And they came with haste, and found Mary, and Joseph, and the babe lying in a manger.

And when they had seen it, they made known abroad the saying which was told them concerning this child.

Look again at what you have read in this book. Then get up from your spiritual place of ease and walk in what you have seen! Like the shepherds who heard the good news of His first coming, go see it—and then tell it!

This and every Christmas, give God something that He can bless! Boldly and without shame, give Him your eyes, your ears, your hands, your feet—your heart.

To all the preachers, reproduce yourself in a people of whom He will not be ashamed. Build something in the name of the Lord that won't have to be burned with fire along with everything else in the Day of the Lord.

It's time for the Messiah! The Seed is the image of God; the Seed is the spirit of prophecy. It's time for Him to live, to speak, to reign! It's time for Christ to be fully formed in His people...all His people...the glorious Church, the Body of Christ!

Mt. 1:21-23, KJV

And she shall bring forth a son, and thou shalt call His name JESUS: for He shall save His people from their sins.

Now all this was done, that it might be fulfilled which was spoken of the Lord by the prophet, saying,

Behold, a virgin shall be with child, and shall bring forth a son, and they shall call His name Emmanuel, which being interpreted is, God with us.

**It's time for the Messiah—
"Emmanuel"—"God with us!"**

(The following spontaneous, prophetic song of the Lord flowed through Pastor Kelley Varner at Praise Tabernacle on Sunday morning, December 17, 1995. It captures the essence of this volume and encourages the reader to get involved with the present move of the Holy Spirit in the earth.)

Emmanuel

For there is born to you this day in the city of our King,
The Lamb of glory. Now to Him we sing.
No one can compare with the Lord so bright and fair,
Emmanuel, God with us.

Let Heav'n and Earth rejoice; Messiah made the choice
To give His life a ransom for us all,
And now the sound goes forth into all the earth.
To young and old, this day He does call.

Nothing can compare with the Babe so bright and fair.
Born so long ago, He came,
But the Babe is now your King, lift your voice and sing,
Jesus Christ, the same.

Let Heav'n and Earth rejoice, Messiah made the choice
To come and give His life for us all,
And now He walks down here, to all who have an ear.
To young and old, this day He calls.

Lift your voice and sing, sing unto your King.
He's the One who died for you.
Nothing can compare with this One so bright and fair;
He's the Way, the Life, the Truth.

Herod could not kill Him, the angels sang His praise
That lovely night so long ago,
Wise men still seek Him, bow down at His feet,
Giving Him the glory we do owe.

Nothing can compare with this One so bright and fair,
The Word made flesh, called a mystery.
But the Babe is now your King, to Him now you can sing,
Your deliverance, your Jubilee!

Emmanuel, Emmanuel, Emmanuel, your King!
Emmanuel, Emmanuel, Emmanuel, to You we sing!

Emmanuel, Emmanuel, Emmanuel, is your King!
Emmanuel, Emmanuel, Emmanuel, to Thee we sing!

Emmanuel, Emmanuel, Emmanuel, is our King!
Emmanuel, Emmanuel, Emmanuel, to You we sing!

Joseph couldn't explain how he felt that night He came,
The wonder of wonders, Jesus is His name,
The holy Seed in Mary manifested in the earth,
The Word made flesh, such a holy birth.

The wonder became a witness, Elisabeth does say.
Mary sang about that day.
Zacharias' tongue was loosed, prophesied about the Lord,
Heaven came to earth, a living Sword.

The wonder became a witness, the shepherds came and saw,
The wonder of, the wonder of it all,
Religious people couldn't understand it, simple country
Shepherds understood the One they worshiped was the Lord.

The witness turned to warfare, Herod's in a rage,
Let's kill that holy Seed, let's put it in a cage!
Let's lock Him up, let's shut Him up,
The world must not hear
That the King of glory, the love of God is come,
The One who casts out fear.

The warfare, it raged, God won the day,
Men in their ignorance can never have their way,
For there is a King set down in Zion. Jesus is His name.
Rejoice, O Israel, He came!

The warfare now is over; the King reigns over all.
Nothing in Heaven and Earth will not respond to His call.
The Word forever settled in Heaven, Jesus the living Word,
Come to Him today now that you've heard.

The warfare became worship, the wise men bowed down,
Gold and Frankincense their store.
We love You, Jesus; You're the Lord of all.
We give You glory, but we're going to give You more.

The gold is the price of worship, a furnace for each one,
To be conformed to the image of the Son.
Frankincense so white, like Him who is so bright.
The purity of worship is in our sight.

But the myrrh is the pain of worship;
You've got to deny yourself, kill your flesh,
Bow down to the Lord of all.
His cross will kill you, put you rightly so to death,
Can anyone hear that call?

The wonder is a witness, the warfare became worship,
Emmanuel, God has come,
Jesus is His name, forever He's the same,
Emmanuel, the most holy One...

Books & Tapes by Kelley Varner

TAPE CATALOG

To receive a full listing of Pastor Varner's books and tapes, write or call for our current catalog:

Praise Tabernacle
P.O. Box 785
Richlands, NC 28574-0785
(910) 324-5026 or 324-5027

TAPE OF THE MONTH

Each month two cassette tapes are made available by Pastor Varner. These messages are ministered by him and others in the fivefold ministry. You may join this growing list of listeners on a monthly offering basis.

VIDEO CASSETTES

We are just beginning this new avenue of ministry. Presently available are three, two-hour video cassettes on the Book of Ruth. This teaching is a verse-by-verse exegesis concerning the Christian walk from conception to perfection, from birth to maturity. Please write or call for more information.

SEMINARS AND CONVENTIONS

There are annual meetings here in Richlands for the Body of Christ. Please inquire for information on the next meeting. There is a team of ministry here at Praise Tabernacle that is available to your local church to teach the principles of restoration and assist in the areas of praise and worship. Please contact Pastor Varner.

Available Tape Series

Jesus, Lord of the Home (12 tapes)
Are You Ready for the Third Dimension? (8 tapes)
Israel: God's Chosen People (8 tapes)
The Kingdom of God (8 tapes)
Spiritual Ministry (12 tapes)
Servant Power (8 tapes)
Four-fold Definition of the Local Church (16 tapes)
The New Testament Local Church (32 tapes)
Halloween, Christmas, Easter (8 tapes)
God's Two Greatest Mysteries (8 tapes)
The Coming of the Lord (12 tapes)
Women's Ministry (8 tapes)
The Book of Acts (8 tapes)
Principles of Kingdom Finance (8 tapes)
Bible Patterns of the Kingdom (12 tapes)
The Faith of God (8 tapes)
The Five-fold Ministry (12 tapes)
Life and Immortality (12 tapes)
Water Baptism (8 tapes)
The Day of Atonement (8 tapes)
Principles of Restoration (12 tapes)
The Will of God (8 tapes)
The Songs of Degrees (16 tapes)
The Emerging Christ (12 tapes)
Apostolic Principles (12 tapes)
Romans, Verse-by-verse (from 8 to 30 tapes)
The Feast of Tabernacles (16 tapes)
The More Excellent Ministry (8 tapes)—these are the original tapes preached at the House of Prayer in 1981

PREVAIL—A HANDBOOK FOR THE OVERCOMER
TPB-196p. ISBN 0-938612-06-9 Retail $8.99

THE MORE EXCELLENT MINISTRY
TPB-280p. ISBN 0-914903-60-8 Retail $9.99

THE PRIESTHOOD IS CHANGING
TPB-238p. ISBN 1-56043-033-8 Retail $8.99

Are you committed to growing in God? Are you seeking greater fulfillment in your fellowship with Him? These books were written for you! In *Prevail* you'll learn three basic ways to be an overcomer. *The More Excellent Ministry* will show you where God's fullness flows unhindered; and *The Priesthood Is Changing* will take you from adolescence to maturity with practical dynamics for growing up! Don't miss even one of these life-changing books!

WHOSE RIGHT IT IS
If Jesus is King and reigns from His throne in Heaven, can the Church abandon the world to satan and wait for their escape from tribulation? Here Pastor Varner carefully examines the Scriptures for a proper perspective on Christ's Lordship and dispensationalism.
TPB-322p. ISBN 1-56043-151-2 Retail $10.99

REST IN THE DAY OF TROUBLE
This book studies in detail the prophecy of Habakkuk. Pastor Varner shows the progression of Habakkuk's expressing his problem to his realizing the provision—and so finding rest in his day of trouble. We too are in a day of trouble and, like Habakkuk, can we find rest in ours?
TPB-294p. ISBN 1-56043-119-9 Retail $9.99

THE ISSUES OF LIFE
Every issue on earth has its answer in the heavens. Spiritual problems require spiritual solutions. The supernatural power and strategic wisdom of the Holy Spirit are no longer an option. The living God is once again intervening in the affairs of men. For the 90's there is only one cry: We must have revival! JESUS IS THE ISSUE!
TPB-182p. ISBN 1-56043-075-3 Retail $8.99

UNSHAKEABLE PEACE
The prophet Haggai's life and words hold a prophetic message for the Body of Christ today. In a detailed study of the Book of Haggai, Pastor Varner presents the *unshakeable peace* that characterizes the Church that Jesus is building!
TPB-252p. ISBN 1-56043-137-7 Retail $8.99